The PROMISE of PRAYER

True Stories from GUIDEPOSTS®
about the Power of Prayer

CRESCENT BOOKS
New York

This 1995 edition is published by Crescent Books, a division of Random House Value Publishing, Inc., 201 East 50th Street, New York, New York 10022,

Crescent Books and colophon are trademarks of Random House Value Publishing, Inc.

Random House
New York • Toronto • London • Sydney • Auckland
http://www.randomhouse.com/

Printed and bound in the United States of America

A CIP catalog record of this book is available from the Library of Congress

ISBN 0-517-10323-0

8 7 6 5

Contents

Introduction

I sought the Lord and he answered me.

PSALM 34.4, NIV

We don't have to use special words to pray—but we do need to ask for the right things. If we pray for God to change our spouses, our families, our friends, our jobs, or our circumstances, He may not do it until we are willing to be changed ourselves. If we pray to have our lives changed, we must be willing to accept whatever new events come our way.

Every genuine prayer gives God a chance to work for us. His power keeps us going in both boring and difficult circumstances. His healing is mysterious, and the stories in this book give us some clues as to how healing comes. Offering ourselves in prayer with others, and at all times—in grave illness and in health, in times of financial troubles or good times—opens the way for God's power to work not only for others but for ourselves.

Although we may be firm believers in the power of

prayer, there are still times when praying is difficult. Life has made such harsh demands that we no longer know what to do. At these times, we must surrender to God and put ourselves in His hands. As Catherine Marshall—one of *Guideposts*'s favorite writers—says, you should "grip with equal strength of will your belief that God can do through you what you cannot. It may seem ... that you are relying on emptiness, danging over a chasm. Disregard these feelings, and quietly thank God that He is working things out." Often we want God to answer our prayers in a specific way—we have a definite idea about what the answer should be. But God's thoughts about what we need are different from ours, and sometimes the answers we receive are unexpected. We are shocked and surprised, but in the process we discover that God doesn't make mistakes. As one woman found out, "Prayer works. It works wonders."

Prayer and Persistence

O Lord God,
when Thou givest to Thy servants to endeavor any great matter,
grant us also to know that it is not the beginning, but the continuing of the same until it be thoroughly finished which yieldeth the true glory;
through Him that for the finishing of Thy work laid down His life.
Amen.

Sir Francis Drake (c.1543–1596)

The Most Needed Virtue

JOSEPH CALDWELL

When my mother died I wanted something that had belonged to her, but not just a memento. I wanted something I could use, so I asked my sisters and brothers if I could have her old missal, the prayer book she took with her to early mass each morning. It was more complete than the one I had. No one objected, and I collected my legacy from the top of her dresser in the upstairs bedroom.

When I got back to New York after the funeral, I looked through the old and tattered book. In it, Mother had inserted special prayers on holy cards, prayers for peace, for missionaries, for friends, for my father who had died eleven years before—a catalog of concerns that she carried with her every day to church, expressions of the faith and hope and love that seemed as much a part of her as the color of her fine brown eyes.

From that old missal, I learned something I had never known about my mother. I'd always thought that her virtues were something she'd been born with, a genetic endowment, so effortless, so pervasive had they been. I can't say I envied her easy goodness; I just took it for granted the way I took for granted the bread she baked and the clothes she sewed. Then, leafing through the missal, I came to a page that was about one-third gone.

This was obviously the page she came to most often, the one she went back to again and again. The edge was yellow and brown where her touch over the years had worn the paper to dust, obscured words and ended sentences in mid-phrase. I looked at the top of the page. It said "Prayer for Perseverance." This, then, was the secret behind her "obvious" goodness; this was the most needed virtue of all, the one that reinforced and nourished all the rest.

I had to smile. The prayer, the words, the page had been worn away by nothing more, nothing less, than perseverance itself. Her prayer, apparently, had been answered

The Man Who Wouldn't Quit

TORIVIO ORTEGA

I had failed again. For the fifth time. I had taken the California bar exam: and for the fifth time I'd failed it. The notification had just come in the mail.

For six years the hope of becoming a lawyer—or being able to do what only an attorney could do for my fellow migrant farm workers—had been a force that drove me. But now, after my fifth failure, I'd run out of gas.

I'd already put too much into the effort—countless hours of studying; precious time stolen from my wife Elena and our two young daughters; scarce, hard-earned dollars that could have gone for things my family needed; too many days and nights of dreaming and hoping.

I sat in our kitchen with the postcard notice in my hand, feeling lower than ever before in my life.

The California bar exam is given twice a year, in February and July, and it takes as long as five months to hear whether you passed. So if a person is going to take it over again, he needs to apply for the next exam right after he finds out he failed the previous one.

Elena, as usual, was full of understanding and encouragement. "You'll just have to try again," she told me.

"No, Elena," I said, the energy and will all drained out of me. "I'm quitting. I've had it."

Then she sat beside me and reminded me of the stories I had told her, experiences out of my childhood and incidents I had witnessed as a young man, things that had influenced me to try to become a lawyer.

I had no trouble remembering them. I'd been born one of six children in a migrant farm worker's family, and for the first eighteen years of my life all I knew was the fields.

It wasn't an easy way to grow up. We chopped cotton in the most sweltering heat. We planted cauliflower in mushy thick clay that, during harvest, can add five pounds to each of your feet as you plod through the rows. I've still got scars on my hands from bucking hay, and my fingernails are still black from artichoke thorns.

Living conditions weren't good either. Sometimes our family would sleep in a single room, empty of furniture, in a labor camp barracks. At other places, we'd sleep in a tent that often had to be put up in a blinding dust storm or a driving rain. Many times we were forced to camp out in the back of my stepfather's old car.

It wasn't so much the hard life, though, that made me want to leave farm work; it was because so few people seemed to care about migrants.

I'll never forget one grower who insisted we climb up

the trees in his orchard to pick dates, even though a strong wind was blowing. If someone had got hurt, it would have been just tough luck for the guy who fell.

Another time I'd gone out to dig potatoes, with a crew that included my mother, and was outraged to find out we were being paid only a dollar a day. When I questioned the grower about the pathetic pay, he laughed and said, "What are you going to do about it?"

There wasn't anything I *could* do, if I wanted a job.

For a while, I escaped all that by joining the army, twice. But each time, when my hitch was over, I drifted back to my own people. I couldn't escape from them.

After my second discharge from the army, in 1968, Elena and I got married, and I landed a job as an aide in the Salinas branch of the Federal Office of Economic Opportunity. Most of the people I dealt with were farm workers. Knowing their plight from personal experience, it felt good when I could help someone with housing, with getting into English language classes, with trying to stabilize a family's life.

But I soon realized there was a lot I couldn't do. When a grower promised to hire so many migrants to pick grapes, then reneged after the workers had shown up for work, many of them traveling a long distance, there was nothing I could lawfully do for the workers left without jobs.

When a group of farm workers told me they didn't want to use shorthandle hoes, which played havoc with a person's back but were favored by the growers, my hands were tied.

Time and time again I saw a migrant charged with something he didn't understand because he spoke only Spanish. I saw workers get into contract disputes and lose because they didn't understand the language. And all I could do was feel angry and frustrated.

Occasionally a worker, more sophisticated than most, would seek legal advice, something he couldn't afford from a private attorney. The legal aid people were sympathetic, but because of their workload and bureaucratic pressures, they seemed unable to improve conditions for the farm workers.

I decided that the migrants needed not just a full-fledged attorney with courtroom ability. They needed someone who cared, someone who understood—as only a person who had shared their life could understand. That was why I had wanted so much to become a lawyer.

I learned that in California you don't need a college degree to get into law school. All you have to do is pass an equivalency test. So in 1974, with the encouragement and advice of Denny Powell, a Salinas attorney and friend, and the support of Elena, I took the test. I was thirty-one years old, had never been to college and had been out of high school since 1959; but I managed to pass the test and was admitted to the nearby Monterey College of Law.

Making it through law school—which I did after four hard years—was only the first big step, though, in becoming an attorney. I also had to pass the state bar exam. And that was the prospect I was now facing—again.

Finally, at Elena's insistence, I agreed to send in an

application for the next exam, to be given in July, but I felt sure I'd never take it. The examination was such an ordeal that just thinking about taking it again depressed me.

I'd have to travel to the city where the exam was to be given, a considerable expense, plus pay the $125 fee for the test. It required two or three nights in a motel, since the exam usually takes three days, working from 8:00 A.M. to 5:00 P.M.

The physical and mental strain is enormous. When you take the exam, you're not allowed to bring in any materials or use the telephone. You are constantly monitored, everywhere—in your seat, in the halls, even in the bathroom. At some point during the exam, and you never know exactly when, you are fingerprinted—a further deterrent against cheating.

The pressure becomes so intense that examinees sometimes simply break down and sob into their exam papers; they just lose control.

I didn't know how to tell Elena that I was going to back out, but I knew I couldn't take it again. I became more and more anxious and confused.

One evening, about three weeks before the test, I left the house to get away for a while. I started walking around our neighborhood, hoping some fresh air would clear my head. Two blocks from home, I came to Sacred Heart Church and stopped in front of it.

Although Elena and the girls attended the church regularly, I hadn't been there in a long time. Constant study and work had kept me from going for several years. Now, when I found the front door open, I went in.

The altar was aglow with soft light and candles, and I crept into a pew at the back of the church and knelt there. I began to think about God and me. I didn't feel that He had let me down by not giving me whatever it took to become what I wanted. Rather, I had the strange feeling that *I* had disappointed *Him* by not trying to find out what *He* wanted for me.

As a boy, I could remember, asking forgiveness from God had always made me feel better. Trying it now, I discovered it still worked. In fact, I felt so much better immediately, I decided to ask God for another favor.

"I need You to tell me something, Lord," I said, clasping my hands in prayer. "I need some kind of sign. I need You to show me whether I should take that test again." After kneeling there for a few minutes longer, without anything happening, I tiptoed out.

The moment I walked outside into the cool, breezy night, my nose twitched at an acrid odor in the air: the smell of fertilizer blowing in from the fields. A green bean crop was being readied somewhere nearby, and the best fertilizer for green bean plants is manure. Only a farm worker would understand that smell, and that was what I smelled now.

Suddenly boyhood memories, sharp and vivid, of dark fields, cold and wet in the predawn hours, came surging back to me. One especially stood out. I could see myself again as a twelve-year-old, moving and stooping in the long rows of beets, working with my parents and brothers and sisters, among other families like us, weeding beets.

We'd begun at six in the morning, when there was a heavy dew on the crops. Within a half hour, I was soaked up to the armpits, freezing cold, and praying for the sun to come up.

"Ma," I said to my mother, who was working alongside me. "Ma, I've had it. I'm going to the car to warm up."

Ma was wet and cold, too, but she wasn't about to stop. To do so would break an unwritten code among migrants. "You don't quit," Ma said, grabbing my arm and sending me back to the beets with a shove. "You don't quit any job till that job's done." I went back to work.

I remembered her determination now. If I really wanted to do something for the farm workers, I had to take that bar exam again—and keep taking it, until I passed. I couldn't quit until the job was done.

"Thank You, Lord," I said, smiling into the darkness.

There was more. Over the next week I continued to ask God for direction. And I got the strongest feeling that I ought to bone up on the law of real property especially, an area I'd had problems with before. I made up my mind I would know it cold, even at the risk of doing poorly in other areas.

With one week remaining before the exam, I somehow knew I had studied enough. Previously I had crammed right up to the final minute, never giving my brain a chance to relax. As a result, I always felt tense and jumpy going into the examination.

Finally, I got an urge to take Elena and the girls with

me to Santa Clara, where the exam was to be given. I had never done that before. I hadn't wanted to be distracted, and I hadn't felt I could afford it. Now I didn't care what it cost; they had sacrificed so much for me. And, I felt I needed them.

On the evening before the first day of the exam, the four of us gathered in our motel room. Marie Elena, our twelve-year-old, announced that they had gifts for me. Pulling a crazy little plastic doll with goofy red hair out from behind her back, Maria Elena told me, "This is to loosen you up, Daddy."

From Katerina, our nine-year-old, I got a four-leaf clover: "For luck, Daddy," she said.

After giving me a big hug, Elena pressed her communion medal into my palm. "For hope," she said tenderly. Tomorrow, I'd be ready.

As with the five other exams, it was hard to tell afterward how I'd done. One thing, though, did give me a lift: there had been questions on real property law, and I knew the answers to all of them.

Then followed five months of waiting for the results, a time of agony. In December, at last, I got my notice. Hallelujah, I passed!

On December 19, 1980, I was admitted to the California Bar. My mother, Elena, the girls and several of our friends came to be with me at the swearing-in ceremony, and I'll bet there wasn't a dry eye in the place.

Three days later I was at work at my new job—as an attorney in the county public defender's office—when a migrant farm worker named Luis was ushered into my office.

Luis, who did not speak English, said he had been charged with vandalism. He didn't do it, he assured me, because he was picking onions at the time. I believed him.

His face weathered and lined from a lifetime in the fields, Luis looked at me sadly and asked in Spanish, "Can you help me?"

I took his hand and gave him the answer we both wanted to hear: *"Si."*

Prayer

BENEDICT OF NURSIA (480–c.547)

O gracious and holy Father,
give us wisdom to perceive Thee,
intelligence to understand Thee,
diligence to seek Thee,
patience to wait for Thee,
eyes to behold Thee,
a heart to meditate upon Thee,
and a life to proclaim Thee;
through the power of the Spirit
of Jesus Christ our Lord.

A David for Today

GRACE RULISON

"David can't learn," the teacher said, tapping a pencil on the desktop in front of her. "He tries hard enough, but I see no alternative but that you take him out of school. I'm sorry."

It was late autumn, 1949. I nodded in silence, my eyes roving along the rows of kindergarten desks. Which one, I wondered, was David's? How would I tell my son he wouldn't be coming back to it?

At eight years of age, David had tried kindergarten three times but had never lasted more than three months. He was only an infant when we noticed something different about our firstborn. He didn't walk or talk as early as other kids. The doctors told us the umbilical cord had been wrapped around David's neck at birth and had cut off his oxygen supply. "His brain damage is severe," explained one doctor. "He'll never assume his own personal care."

Yet as David grew, I couldn't get over a strong sense

that his situation was not hopeless. Physically he was learning to take care of his personal needs. Maybe, just maybe, he could overcome some of his mental shortcomings too.

So for several years my husband, Everett, and I sent David to school, and the school sent David back home.

Standing that day in David's classroom, I wondered if I had been wrong to think David could learn. Was I living in a land of dreams, a land where underdogs could win the day and little boys could slay giants as another David, with a slingshot, had slain Goliath? All I knew was that my hope was almost gone.

We talked to the school psychologist. "Mr. and Mrs. Rulison," he said, "I suggest that you arrange custodial care for your son in a state institution for the mentally retarded. In David's case, it's the only thing you can do."

Grimly we drove to the institution for a visit. We walked through the long halls, passing a white-uniformed woman leading a line of boys David's age to the bathroom. The sight tore at my heart. At once, the conviction that David could learn came surging back. "David doesn't belong here," I blurted, wondering where such knowledge came from.

Even though it was expensive and we had four other children to raise, Everett and I found a private boarding school in another city that would take David in and try to teach him.

As I packed David's belongings, he tugged at my sleeve. "Mom, why do I have to go away?"

"So you can have a chance to learn, David. Don't you want to read?"

His nod was vigorous. More than anything, David wanted to learn to read. To count, to name the colors of the rainbow, to tell time. I thought of him, staring at the face of our kitchen clock, trying to decipher its complexity of numbers and moving hands. How my son wanted to learn, to understand! And, I thought, how the rest of us take the joy of learning for granted.

Meanwhile, problems were developing in my own life. A series of physical symptoms cropped up that no one could diagnose. When doctors finally discovered the problem, I heard one of them tell Everett, "I'm afraid it's too late." I was admitted to the hospital in the last stages of intestinal cancer.

Clutching my husband's hand, I lay in bed. What would become of my family? What would happen to David? Our minister appeared at my bedside. "Grace, you have a ring of prayer around you," he said. Those words fell around me like a life preserver.

In the days that followed, I felt buoyed up by God's love, filled with hope that I could beat the cancer. Resting on that "ring of prayer," I let go, placing my life in God's hands. Slowly, I began to get well, and eventually I went back home to a normal life.

But the medical bills had mounted and we could no longer keep David at the private school. At home, I struggled to teach him myself. Each morning he'd follow his brothers and sisters to the school bus, then shuffle back up the drive, kicking a rock. Inside, he'd sit on the edge of his chair, impatient for his lesson to begin.

"What's this?" I'd ask, pointing to a word.

Hunched forward, he'd study the letters the same way he studied the kitchen clock, his little boy's face scrunched with effort—but it was no use.

"I don't know," he'd whisper.

I'd take him in my arms, feeling his small body nestled against mine, and try not to give in to despair.

A ring of prayer. When I'd faced my own death, hadn't that been my strongest weapon? Leaning back onto a circle of trust and giving my plight to God had saved my life. Could it save David's too?

I smoothed back the brown hair on my son's forehead and let go, trusting God to help David as He'd helped me: in His own time, in His own way. I explained to David that he needed to pray, to trust God. Together, we would accept what David couldn't do, and thank God for what he could do.

That year, special education started in the schools, making it possible for David to return to the classroom. It was there that a kind man named Mr. Mercer came into his life. Mr. Mercer was the school custodian. David, whose social skills were never in question, made a habit of stopping by the janitor's closet for a visit after school.

"Can you tell time?" David asked one day.

"Why, sure," said Mr. Mercer. "Can you?" David shook

his head. The next day, Mr. Mercer was waiting with a "learning clock."

Every day after school, he spent time with David, patiently and carefully working with him. Again and again, for months, he'd hold up the clock and ask David, "What time is it?" Mr. Mercer was never discouraged when David couldn't answer, and he wouldn't let David get discouraged either. "You'll get it, son," he'd say. "Let's try again."

Then one day David came running home from school, pointed at the kitchen clock, and almost shouted, "It's a quarter to four!"

And so it was.

It was David's first real breakthrough into learning, and he was so proud! He'd go around telling perfect strangers the time of day. I bought him a watch, which I taught him to wind. Every night, carefully, he'd take it off and lay it right by his pillow.

The ring of prayer—it was holding David up.

As David grew into his teens, his hunger to learn seemed bottomless. But at seventeen, no longer eligible for special education, he still could not recognize more than a few words. He was wonderful, though, at telling time.

He got a job as a hospital dishwasher, but evenings and weekends were torture—dark stretches of boredom, loneliness and depression. I would hear him in his room: "God, send someone to help me. Please help me to read, help me to learn."

One by one, David's brothers and sisters married and

left home. "Will I get married?" he'd ask. He was so full of love that I ached at his question. As I gently tried to explain that marriage wouldn't likely be part of his future, he would grow quiet. *"Why* did I have to have brain damage?" he'd ask. *"Why?"*

One Sunday morning after services, I stood talking with one of the women in our church. Before I knew it, I was telling her how eager my mentally handicapped son was to learn, but that he seemed incapable.

"You should hear him pray for help," I told her. "Afterward he waits for something, anything. It's agonizing. Here he is, well past twenty, and he can't get beyond a first-grade level." Evelyn Hoeldtke listened quietly, until finally I said, "I'm running on so about David ..."

She smiled. "I'm a retired schoolteacher. Maybe I can help somehow."

Soon after, Evelyn came up to David and me at church. "I'd like to tutor you, David," she said. "It's time to get on with your education." I noticed David's chin quiver a bit, but above it was just about the widest grin I'd ever seen.

Every Saturday I drove David to Evelyn's house for his lesson. They started with a first-grade reader, a numbers book and a social studies workbook. After each session David's shirt was sweat-soaked with effort. But his effort always outweighed his progress.

David never let up, not once. And neither did this remarkable woman, who refused pay, saying simply that David needed her help. No longer were evenings and weekends awful for David; he spent them poring over his books.

One night as he tried for the thousandth time to piece together the words on a page, his face lit up. "The cat ran up the tree," he said out loud. He looked at me, his face shining. *"The cat ran up the tree!"* I had never heard such beautiful words.

Almost immediately David started to recognize and spell hundreds of words. Suddenly he was reciting rhymes, taking measurements, multiplying by two, using a calculator. His progress was astonishing. Once again I overheard him praying. "God, You are so good to me." The very same prayer was in my heart too.

David's world came alive. He blossomed with a new confidence, becoming a church usher, joining a bicycle club, cycling with his new friends on trips. At the hospital, he was allowed to put up the pantry stock since he could read almost all the labels. That pleased him to no end. One day I opened the hospital newspaper to see David's picture with a caption that read, "Employee of the Month." I could not quit staring at it.

One evening after work he waltzed through the door and said, "Mom, I found a friend."

"Who is he?" I asked.

David grinned. *"Her* name is Caryn, and she accepts me just like I am."

I looked at him, speechless, as he bubbled over with the news. "I met her at the bicycle rack at the mall. I told her my name and asked her to go to the movies. She said yes."

Was this just David's wishful thinking? The following week, sure enough, a lovely young woman arrived at our

door. She'd come to pick up David, she said.

Caryn was a store clerk in her midtwenties, studying nights at the University of South Florida to become a social worker. Full of warmth and a special kind of maturity, she befriended David. Not once did I see her embarrassed by his childlike ways.

Eighteen months after they met, David bicycled down to the jewelry store and bought a diamond ring, arranging to pay a bit each month from his dishwasher's salary. "I'm going to ask Caryn to marry me," he announced, showing me the sparkling jewel.

I bit my lip, knowing what a terrible disappointment he was in for. But I couldn't bring myself to dash his enthusiasm.

When Caryn brought him home after their next date, I looked at her finger—and caught my breath. She was wearing his ring!

"She said yes!" David was shouting.

When we had a moment alone, I looked into Caryn's eyes. "You know David's limitations," I said. "Are you sure?"

"We *all* have limitations," said Caryn. "David and I are in love, and we have a lot to give to each other." After that I had no more doubts. They were married in St. Paul's Lutheran Church in a big, beautiful wedding.

That was several years ago, and today they happily share each other's lives. They studied together until David passed his driver's license test. Now, with his own truck, he supplements his hospital salary with an aluminum-can recycling business that he started himself.

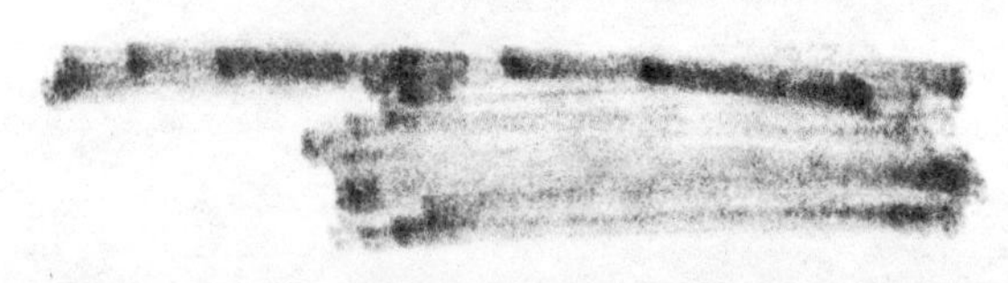

I know I sound like the proud mother, but I can't help marveling at my son. He has pushed himself far beyond anyone's expectations. Just seeing how far he's come gives me strength to face my own toughest problems. For he never stopped fighting, and he never stopped believing that God would help him. There is a ring of prayer that will help you fight the stiffest odds. If you let go and trust your situation to God, He will help you—in His own time and His own way—to overcome what can be changed and to accept what cannot.

The other day, David parked his brand-new truck outside my house and bounded through the door. "It's a quarter to six," he said, with a look at the old kitchen clock. And thinking of the little boy who'd struggled so hard to read that clock, I smiled.

This David had taken on his own Goliath, and won.

"I'm a Firm Believer in Prayer"

JOCELYN M. BRADLEY

When my father, Claude Bradley, tried to get out of bed that morning, his legs and feet felt as if they were still asleep. Soon the numbness began spreading through the rest of his body. My mother summoned help, and Dad was driven to the hospital.

Dad's condition finally was diagnosed as a severe stroke. "This was a bad one, Mr. Bradley," his doctor said. "You'll probably never walk again."

But the doctors didn't know my father. Dad returned home, began exercising and in three days regained use of the right half of his body and his left arm. He bought crutches and began a grueling therapy program. Three months later, having regained the use of his left leg, he threw away his crutches and switched to a walking cane. In two weeks the cane, too, was discarded. His gait may be slow, and permanent paralysis in his left foot causes a limp, but Dad walks on his own!

When his baffled doctors asked "How?" Dad didn't mince words. "I'm a firm believer in prayer. I did all I could on my own, and I asked God to do the rest. And, gentlemen, as you can see, I did my part and He did His, and here I am."

Prayer

Give me, O Lord, a steadfast heart,
which no unworthy affection may drag downwards;
give me an unconquered heart,
which no tribulation can wear out;
give me an upright heart,
which no unworthy purpose may tempt aside.

THOMAS AQUINAS (1225–1274)

PRAYER THAT'S SPECIFIC

A Prayer

Give me a good digestion, Lord,
   And also something to digest;
But when and how that something comes
   I leave to Thee, Who knowest best.

Give me a healthy body, Lord;
   Give me the sense to keep it so;
Also a heart that is not bored
   Whatever work I have to do.

Give me a healthy mind, Good Lord,
   That finds the good that dodges sight:
And, seeing sin, is not appalled,
   But seeks a way to put it right.

. . .

Give me a sense of humour, Lord,
   Give me the power to see a joke,
To get some happiness from life
   And pass it on to other folk.

THOMAS HENRY BASIL WEBB (1898–1917)

A Black-Cat Tale

BARBARA BILLINGSLEY MOHLER

Sometimes, as the saying goes, there's the last straw. And then sometimes there's ... the last *cat!* The time of the last cat had come to our household. Our latest house cat, Pajamas, had disappeared, and when it became clear that he'd never return, I said to my two youngest children, "That's it, kids. No replacement. No more cats."

Now, my declaration may have seemed coldhearted, but I felt I had good grounds. Cats had brought me nothing but trials. Judy ... Bounce ... Little Angel ... Quigley ... Duffy. I was tired of the whole thing. As a single parent with young children, I had enough to worry about. I didn't need to be dashing to the grocery store for pet food ... combing the area at midnight for another wayward tabby. I'd had it. No more cats!

Well, I repeated my declaration until I was nearly blue in the face, and still my Sherman, then ten, and Ginger, seven, wouldn't give up their hopes. A month went by and they never failed to make me aware of whose cats in the area had had kittens. And it appeared that practically *every* family had kittens to spare.

Finally I came up with one of my bright ideas. "Kids," I said, "let's pray about it and lay a fleece before the Lord." They avidly agreed.

By saying "fleece," I was of course invoking the example of Gideon's fleece, from Judges 6:36–40. In that passage, Gideon asks God, as a sign of assurance, to soak a fleece with dew while the ground all around remains dry. And the Lord did just that. It shames me a little to say so, but I think I was about to make a deliberately outlandish request.

"Lord," I prayed, "the children feel that we should have a cat. I disagree, so we are coming to You for direction. Father, if we are to have a cat, I am asking You to have a kitty walk up our pathway straight to our door. Amen."

"And, Lord," added Ginger, "please make him black." Her addition didn't worry me. By now I was sure my prayer was sufficiently *un*answerable.

More than a month went by. No cat. I figured I was in the clear ... until the day I walked across the street to visit with a friend. As I rang her doorbell—with my back turned to my own house—I heard hysterically gleeful cries behind me.

"Mom, Mom, Mom! Look, look, look!"

I turned to look back. There, wobbling up my pathway, was a tiny kitty. A *black* kitty no less. The Word of God says "faint not." I tried not to. The kids started jumping up and down. "Thank You, Jesus," they cried.

My friend opened her door just as the black kitty walked through *my* door. "I can't believe this," she laughed, having learned earlier of my ruse. "That's the Lord's Cat."

And so he was ... and still is at age eleven. Named "Meow-buddy," he has never run away, never gotten stuck in trees, never clawed my upholstery, and is, most amazingly, agreeable to any and all kinds of cat food. I guess you could call our black cat golden.

The Miracle of Asking

JOSE CASSERES

I had paused briefly under the portico of the old church to button my overcoat against the biting December rain. Who could ever guess the extraordinary reason that had brought me fifty blocks uptown from my Wall Street office on a day like this? As I wrestled with the facts, I tried to convince myself that the whole thing made sense.

Over that weekend, twenty-five of us belonging to the Young Marrieds Fellowship of the Marble Collegiate Church had gone to a retreat center fifty miles away from New York City. It had been a time for fellowship, meditation and prayer.

Then on Saturday night, responding to the challenge of a young attorney, we'd agreed to a daring experiment. For six months, with no strings attached, no holding back, we would surrender to God the most compelling need in our lives. With lawyerlike precision, he outlined the terms of our agreement. We were unreservedly to put our most heartfelt need in God's hands, praying daily for one another as well as ourselves.

To seal our agreement, we wrote out this need on a slip of paper and placed it in a self-addressed envelope. "As you write this down," he said, "pray that this desire will lodge itself deeply in your subconscious mind." The church secretary would be asked to mail the envelopes back to us in six months. My job was to deliver those twenty-five envelopes to the church. I now faced my own secret doubts.

"How," I asked myself, "would our group of spiritual novices ever maintain the serious discipline of prayer and faith necessary for such an experiment?" For although the group had met every other Tuesday for several years, most of the experienced ones had moved away, and their places had been taken by others, eager for spiritual discovery, but beginners nonetheless.

Back in the office, I faced the mountain of detailed paper work that is my daily fare in the export-import business. Then, as that day spilled over to the next and the next and the weeks eased into months, all thought of the experiment slipped from my mind.

I was diverted, not only by the computer-paced life of the city with its endless demands for my time and attention, but I also became increasingly overwhelmed by worry and fear over my job. My boss and I seemed locked in a ceaseless conflict over company policy. Our verbal fist fights became a daily occurrence. What began as mere disagreement mushroomed into a full-scale war.

Finally one day the tension reached the boiling point.

He exploded. I exploded. Furious, I walked out of the office and down the hall, searching frantically for momentary seclusion and a chance to cool off. In desperation I locked myself in an empty office. On my knees, I pleaded, "O God, give me an answer to this!"

Within minutes I felt under control. A strange inner calm encompassed me. I walked back down the hall to the boss's office to get my paycheck. And then I got the news. I was fired—as of that moment. Curiously there was still no panic, no fear, not even resentment. Instead, I felt relieved.

With calm precision—although I was keenly aware of what it meant to be out of a job in the middle of a recession—I cleaned out my desk and headed home. As if under someone else's direction, I found myself at the stationery store buying a typewriter. Once home, the realization dawned on me. *This is what I've always wanted—a chance to be self-employed. Today I start my own export-import business.*

I cleared my desk to make room for the new typewriter. And that's when I saw it. The dime-store envelope, self-addressed, lying face up on the top of the day's mail, the letter I had mailed to myself six months before. I ripped it open. There in my own handwriting was my earnest plea—"the courage to start my own business."

Was it coincidence or an answer to prayer? My mind telescoped to that Saturday night meeting. Could there possibly be any connection between today's events and that long-forgotten request we'd made to God? There was only one way to find out—to hear the reports of the others at next Tuesday night's meeting. Finally the appointed hour for the meeting arrived. Seated informally about the room were sixteen of the original twenty-five.

After a brief prayer, I opened the meeting, reciting, as calmly as possible, the circumstances that had led to my self-employment. I didn't have too much time to gauge the group's reaction before Gerry Mengel was talking.

His strawberry blond, freshly grown mustache moved as he blurted out his story. "I have to confess," he started, "like Jose, I forgot all about our prayer pact, but that's what makes my story even more amazing."

He began by reminding us that at the time of the retreat he'd been given just six months to find a new job. Prodded into action by some of the men in our group, he'd finally written a resume and set up appointments for interviews. Then just a few days before our meeting, his boss called him in with startling news. They'd found a spot for Gerry in their Philadelphia office. Believe it or not, the very day he got this news he'd gone home to find his own self-addressed envelope. It's message? "How can I get a job in Philadelphia, so I can be close to my family?"

Betsy Lehman, a tall, poised school nurse, was talking. Six months ago, her situation had seemed hopeless. Released at midyear in an "economy move," she had sought positions in a number of places without success. She had printed in large letters on her slip of paper just one word, "job." Recently she told us she had unexpectedly been offered a much more challenging position teaching nursing at a local college. At first she'd been scared, but like me, she was relishing this new opportunity.

Jim Wightman, a salesman, was the next to report. As far as I knew Jim had never uttered a prayer in his life. He was the newest member of the group and just seemed to sit quietly in each meeting absorbing it all. But now he came to life.

Like me, Jim had lost his job only to discover that it was a blessing in disguise. Not only had he been led to start a new career in mutual funds, which he was finding highly rewarding but the whole experience had also brought his family together. His wife was helping at home, doing a lot of his secretarial and telephone work. The kids were even hand-addressing circulars. Jim was exuberant.

Not all the answers to prayer involved jobs. One advertising man told how he and his wife had learned to communicate better. Others told of relationships that had straightened out.

Sally Jamieson, a grade school teacher, was the last to report. She had been our resident skeptic, always asking us to demonstrate the reality of our faith, demanding us to "prove it." Annoying as this had sometimes been, we all knew we needed it; Sally kept us honest.

In her clipped New England accent Sally told of her answer. "It happened," she said, "the very day I received my envelope."

The teachers of the school where Sally worked had had their monthly meeting that afternoon. Typically, these meetings were full of rancor. Nobody trusted anyone else, there were rigidly maintained factions, the principal was indecisive and little was accomplished. But on this magical day things had been different. People had listened to each other. Decisions which had been postponed for months were finally made. The principal had shown new courage and had taken a stand on some important issues. By the end of the meeting, everyone in the room was aware of a new sense of community, a new respect for each other as people. It all seemed like a miracle, she said.

When she got home and opened the day's mail, Sally was stunned. She read what she had asked for six months before: "Closer cooperation and teamwork among the teachers."

It was an incredible meeting—and an incredible report. What had happened really? We were spiritual neophytes, untrained in matters of faith, undisciplined in prayer. We had solemnly agreed on a prayer pact and some of us had done better than others. Yet despite our inconsistency, God had honored our prayer requests. Why?

None of us had a good answer. Yet in looking back we have learned a few things. In the first place, the long-ago Saturday night session, when we searched our hearts and offered our greatest need to God, was power-packed. We meant business and God knew it. And our prayers that night helped each of us to see our heart's desire clearly and fix it firmly in our subconscious minds. Even though our conscious minds were more aware of day-to-day problems, the prayer was continuing in the back of minds.

There is another explanation. When we go to God unreservedly with our deepest need and what we desire is in our best interest, He is eager to help us. The reason is simple; He loves us.

The House That Was All I Could Have Asked For—and the Funny Thing Is, I Did

ELLEN AKERS

In 1972 my husband began working on a new job in Winnemucca, Nevada. Returning to our home in California from a weekend house-hunting trip in that area, I felt terribly discouraged. No money to buy a house, nothing available to rent. I flopped into a chair in the dining room and gazed despondently out the window. *What now?* I thought.

My mind began to churn. Wasn't God supposed to help people in trouble? What did I really know about God anyway? I had taught children in Sunday school that God is love; that He cares. But was I really sure? Did He care about a home for my family and me? Did He *really* care? Now was the time to find out. I got down on my knees.

I poured out my frustrations and hopes that Monday morning in my dining room in California.

"O Father, after so many years of tiny houses, I would just love something bigger—at least a living room and four bedrooms. Our two boys could each have a bedroom and I could have a sewing room."

The more I thought about it, the more excited I became. My mind ran ahead of my words as I visualized the little things that would mean so much to me. "A big yard and lots of trees. It would have to be terribly cheap rent because we're so broke right now and I really don't care how old and beat-up it is—just an old barn would be fine!"

All week I had such a feeling of anticipation and excitement—like a little girl with a big secret. I didn't know what would happen, but I could sure dream.

The following Monday morning I was sitting in the same old chair, and the thought occurred to me that quietly, inside myself, I could dedicate a part of this dream house to God. But what part? "Father," I began a little sheepishly, "if there were *five* bedrooms, we could use that extra one for a foster child or anyone who needed a home. But You know that my husband has never been much for having people in our home for long periods of time, so You'll have to work it out with him."

That afternoon the phone rang. It was my husband Ray calling from Winnemucca. We had talked about how nice it would be to have four bedrooms but he knew nothing about my five-bedroom prayer, let alone all the details.

He was quite excited and said, "Just listen to this. I was walking down the main street today and I saw a 'house for sale' sign in the window of Glenn's Camera Shop. I went in and asked about it. He said I probably wouldn't be interested because it was sort of an old barn. But I wanted to see it anyway, so we went up just to look. As soon as I saw it I knew you'd like it."

"And it has five bedrooms, right?" I quipped.

"Yes, it does," he answered quickly, then hurried on to tell me more of the details of his find. "The living room is thirty feet long and there's a big yard, lots of trees, a large garage, laundry porch, all those bedrooms. It's not in real good shape, but we can take care of that later."

I stood there trying to get things organized in my mind. Was this *the house?* No waiting, no trials?

"But we have no money," I said.

"Oh, that's all worked out," Ray rushed on. "Glenn is financing it for us at payments we can afford and my old truck will be the down payment. We can draw up the papers this afternoon and sign them in the morning—that is, if you don't mind buying the house without seeing it." Then he added cautiously, "Honey, you know the fellow I've been staying with here? Would it be okay with you if he came and stayed with us for a while? We do have that extra bedroom."

The next morning, one day after I'd said the five-bedroom prayer, the house was in our name.

A few weeks later I made a trip to Winnemucca to see the house. I pulled up in front of it and prepared to feast my eyes. It was just an old blue house with a lilac bush trying to leap over the fence, but it was beautiful to me. My heart went up in joy as I thanked God.

As we settled into our new house further blessings revealed themselves—a lot of them things that could only have meaning for me: a playhouse for the kids; producing fruit trees so that I could can; a wonderful nook in the kitchen; a cubbyhole in the entry hall that is just right for my potbellied stove.

When the extra bedroom was empty again, we arranged to keep three small foster children in our home. Tracy and Theresa were blond, blue-eyed, three-year-old twins. Veronica was their tiny sister.

God continues to work in our family now that we depend on Him. And I'm sure He has provided us this old blue house so we might do His work, too, sharing our love and our home with those He sends to us. For now I know He cares about His children, He really does, down to the last detail.

Prayer

God, give me sympathy and sense,
And help me keep my courage high.

God, give me calm and confidence,
And please—a twinkle in my eye!

MARGARET BAILEY

PRAYING WITH OTHERS

The Day Thou Gavest Lord Is Ended

. . .

We thank Thee that Thy Church unsleeping
While earth rolls onward into light,
Through all the world her watch is keeping,
And rests not now by day or night.

As o'er each continent and island
The dawn leads on another day
The voice of prayer is never silent
Nor dies the strain of praise away.

JOHN ELLERTON (1826–1893)

The Park Ridge, New Jersey, Experiment

ROBERT MILLER

I've always believed that God gives us cues for living, cues that we must be on the alert for, or we miss them. Over the years, those cues have directed my life in many major decisions: my faith, my choice of career, my marriage. In October 1980, God sent me another cue that I picked up on. It changed my life. And the lives of some friends of mine.

I remember it was a Thursday night; I had just returned to my room at the Los Angeles Hilton, exhausted from three intensive business meetings. As manager for a large communications corporation in New York, I had flown to the West Coast to coordinate a major equipment cutover for one of our customers. It was a complex job. I had always loved my work, but lately it seemed there was just one crisis after another.

While waiting to join my associates for dinner, I picked up a copy of *Guideposts* that the hotel provides for its guests. The story I opened to was about some men in

Cincinnati who had business, unemployment or family problems but who found solutions after taking part in a "prayer experiment." I'm a committed Catholic layman—as a young man I had even felt called to be a priest—and I believe in prayer. So I found this story about ordinary laymen like me who used faith to solve practical problems intriguing. But then I went to dinner and forgot about it.

The next day on the plane, when I put my hand in my attaché case I came up with that copy of *Guideposts* again. Strange, I hadn't intended to take it with me; I must have picked it up inadvertently with my business papers.

"The Prayer Experiment." The bold red title leaped out at me. I had opened to that same article. Well, before I knew it, I'd read that story *again.* It was about a middle-aged architect, Herb Hilmer, whose business was failing. It seems he heard about a prayer group called The Pittsburgh Experiment, which has been ministering to businessmen since 1952. Hilmer and an unemployed friend prayed for each other's problems for thirty days. By the last day both men had been helped. That was the beginning of what today is The Cincinnati Experiment.

Could it be so simple? I wondered. *And why am I reading this article again?* At the end of the story there was an editorial note inviting readers to form their own Experiment groups. A nationwide organization was forming called The Guideposts National Experiment.

Back home in Park Ridge, New Jersey, the next morning, after sleeping late, I was romping on my bed with three of my kids when the phone rang. It was Rich DiLeo, an acquaintance, an enterprising young executive. At least he *had* been. "Bob, I've lost my job," he said. "I hate to bother you, but are there any openings at your office?"

I get a lot of calls from people with problems, because I'm involved in help-groups at our parish church. But this surprised me.

"Hey ... I'll work cheap, Bob," Rich quipped.

"We don't have a thing, Rich, I'm sorry," I replied. "Say ... try Jack Funesti." Jack, a mutual friend, was the vice-president of a perfume company.

"I tried him. Didn't you know? He's out of work, too."

"No ... I didn't," I said. "But what about George Barker? I'll bet he'll ..."

"Bob, where have you been?" Rich said, his voice now flat. "Barker lost his job six weeks ago."

That shook me. Three friends, all of them out of work! Then it hit me: *The story in* Guideposts *had mentioned unemployed men!* It sent goose bumps down my back.

Five minutes later I was in the kitchen, excitedly telling my wife June and one of our seven kids about Rich's call and the *Guideposts* story. "What an uncanny coincidence," June said.

"Honey, it was no coincidence," I said. "I'm sure the Lord was telling me something, but what?"

The next day at mass I prayed for an answer—one that wasn't long in coming. That afternoon while I was watching NFL football on TV, an idea popped into my head: *Why not write to The National Experiment?* The address was there in the *Guideposts* article. Then I wrote notes to those men who had lost their jobs, and to a few I had heard of in the meantime. I invited them over to my house on Thursday. I even wrote a note to Hugh Tuomey, a high school friend I hadn't seen in ten years. That was a foolish-seeming whim, but I mailed the letter anyway.

The whole thing was crazy. What was I getting myself into? *I* wasn't unemployed ... I wasn't even sure what I'd do or say at that meeting.

The day before our get-together, a packet of literature arrived from The National Experiment—just in time!

On Thursday, my whole family got into the act. June made coffee and cookies; the kids hung around to help me greet the fellows at the door. Six men showed up—not bad for starters. Dennis, my son-in-law, had dropped by. He was having trouble with *his* job, so he stuck around, too.

Just before we began, I told my old classmate Hugh, "Maybe this isn't for you. I don't know what your situation is ..."

"Bob," he replied, enthusiastically, "I've just changed jobs, and I think I've made a big mistake. I'm working with a bunch of *sharks.* How did you know I needed help?"

"I didn't," I replied.

As we settled down, there were jokes about résumés and being obsolete at forty, but once the meeting began, those men I had invited into my home were looking at me intently. They expected—*needed*—to hear me say something that would help them. I sent up a hurried prayer ...

Beginning the meeting, I said, "This may be crazy, but we're here to try an experiment in prayer." Then I went over The National Experiment guidelines with them. We had to *accept* one another—"as we are, where we are." We had to be *honest* with one another, *sharing* our failures, our successes, our pain. We had to *trust* and *encourage* one another. There should be no criticism or attempts to give "advice."

We introduced ourselves. Each man told something about his situation. From the start we really tried to stay loose and let the Lord take over the meeting. And we felt His presence there, especially in the pauses, the silences. This in itself was unusual, because business executives are so "task oriented" that ordinarily we want to fill up every second with activity or talk.

"You know," Hugh said, after one of these pauses, "I like this sharing business, because when you're down and out you tend to focus on yourself and your own problems. Your fear isolates you, cuts you off. You begin to think you're the only guy in the whole world who's out of work. But it says here the Experiment requires that you pray about the *other* man, care about him. I think that's healthy."

Before the meeting concluded, each man was assigned a "prayer buddy"—a man he'd pray for, and who would in turn pray for him, daily, for thirty days. We agreed to meet each Thursday at my home at 8:00 P.M. to share results.

Things began to happen. Not suddenly, like magic, but gradually. As the weeks passed, men who had been bitter and withdrawn or whose boisterous laughter had masked anxiety, talked about their innermost fears and hopes. In the very act of sharing there was a kind of healing. We were experiencing the truth of St. Paul's words: "... to comfort those who are in any affliction, with the comfort with which we ourselves are comforted by God." (2 Corinthians 1:4, RSV).

And what were the results? Here are some of them:

Chuck Garrison: Chuck, like me, had a job, but he had been unfairly passed over for promotion; he felt stagnant on his job and needed a challenge. We really prayed for Chuck. Over a period of weeks you could see the change in him, as he learned that he wasn't the only man who had ever been given a raw deal. Within five weeks of joining the Experiment he made a renewed commitment to the Lord. Then, quite suddenly, Chuck received not one but several good job offers. We were amazed at the almost immediate response to our prayers for Chuck.

George Barker: George was one of the three unemployed executives who had started me on this whole Experiment. Within a few weeks of starting the Experiment, George received a job offer and relocated in Indiana. Again we were amazed at the quick results, and so was George. Yet, within a month, he called to say things weren't working out at all.

What had gone wrong? Nothing, actually. We were learning that God doesn't always move us in a straight line to our goal. He may want us to have learning experiences along the way. At any rate, we put George back on our prayer list. Within another month or so, he received a new job offer in Washington, D.C. He's been there over a year now, and he and his family are happy and settled in. But it took lots of prayer and patience.

Jack Funesti: Jack was a vice-president who had been forced into early retirement. For years his hobby had been making picture frames. One night he confided to us: "Now that I've got time on my hands I've been wondering if I could do it professionally—you know, open a little frame shop." His eyes as he spoke were shining.

"Sounds like something you really want to do, Jack," I said. "Let's all be praying about it. Okay?"

Our prayers and support gave Jack the courage to take the plunge, to step out in faith to do the thing he had always dreamed of. Eventually he opened that little frame shop. Today, a year later, it's thriving. And so is Jack.

John Doris: A bright guy who had lost one job because of a chronic back problem and was about to lose another. Like many troubled men, John's instinct was to crawl away and hide like a wounded animal. One night his wife called to say that John had been hospitalized for back surgery. "Bob, will you ask the men to pray for him, please ... ?" I assured her we would.

Later, when the doctors were "prepping" John for surgery, they discovered that his back condition had "somehow" improved so dramatically that they canceled the operation! Today, John is well and has begun his own business. He is a core member of the Experiment, and one of our most vocal supporters. Not only did the Lord provide John with a job, but He restored his health, too.

I could go on and on with stories. Of course it would be misleading to imply that every man has had a perfect answer. God never promised riches or a long-term retirement plan, though He always supplies manna for the day. Some of our members have had to give up Cadillacs and caviar but all of us in this fellowship of like-minded men are learning humility, patience and the secret of letting God direct our lives.

It's been remarkable, this experiment in prayer. In the past twenty-two months twenty-one unemployed men have joined us. *Eighteen* of those men have found jobs! (We're currently busy on the other three!) So you see, it's worked for us. It can work anywhere—it can work in your town, with your friends, associates, neighbors—with *you*.

And what of me? I'm still working hard at my job, still being challenged. But I've found that reaching out to help others, and depending on the Lord for answers, has greatly lessened the stress and strain of my own work. That's what the Experiment is about, too—helping *employed* men cope with job pressures in the workplace.

I know that the feeling of pressure I had the night I first read about the Experiment in the hotel room has vanished. That was the night that God gave me a cue—I'm glad I didn't miss it.

Me, Lead a Prayer Group?

CLAIRE DONCH

In the winter of 1982–83 my husband Mike and I were in deep financial trouble. We had a lot of bills to pay, especially my own medical ones, and things had gotten so bad we were forced to accept food from my church and money from the local Christmas fund to buy our little girl Heidi a winter coat.

We weren't the only ones. We live in Erie, Pennsylvania, a town of a hundred twenty thousand. In spite of the corporate presence in Erie of General Electric, Hammermill Paper and Bucyrus-Erie, the unemployment rate was 18 percent! Mike worked for a cable TV company on commission; he received no regular salary, and though he was working more than fifty hours a week, his paychecks continually dwindled. So on weekends he worked as a saxophonist with a band, and I had a part-time job. But still, with the steady drain of a big medical bill and several other unexpected setbacks, we couldn't make it. Our problem was not *un*employment but *under*employment.

The day I returned from shopping for Heidi's coat, Mike came home for lunch with his co-worker Randy Weed. Randy enjoyed eating at our house; soup and sandwiches were a break from the macaroni-and-cheese he and his family were subsisting on. Mike had had a bad morning. Out of twenty-five calls, not one person had subscribed to the cable system. And while Mike was on his home-visiting rounds, one guy had actually thrown him off a porch.

I was heartsick as I made the sandwiches. As humiliating as it was accepting charity, at least we had been able to get Heidi's present. But it would be a slim Christmas at Randy's house. All at once I felt like crying—for us, for Randy's kids, for all the decent, hard-working families struggling in the recession that gripped the nation.

A few days after the shopping expedition, the November 1982 issue of *Guideposts* arrived. One of the articles in the new issue grabbed me. Titled "The Park Ridge, New Jersey, Experiment," it was about Robert Miller, a Christian businessman who started a prayer group with unemployed friends. I wondered if this sort of group could work for Mike, because the Experiment story told how good things began to happen for Bob Miller and his friends as they prayed together about their common problems. Most of them found jobs; all were strengthened and comforted.

When Mike got home that night I asked him to read the Miller story. He didn't want to at first. Mike, who's a church-going Catholic, believed that *Guideposts* was for—

and about—Protestants. (I myself am Protestant, a member of Wesley United Methodist.) I persisted and Mike finally read Bob Miller's story.

Initially he wasn't impressed. But the next day he went back and read the story again. A nagging feeling told him he had missed something; it was that Bob Miller, too, was Roman Catholic. They had something in common. And Mike related to the problems of the men in the story. True, he had a job, but the financial stresses were the same.

I was surprised when Mike suggested that we write to the Guideposts National Experiment, the organization that gave Bob Miller's group its guidelines.

Soon we received a letter back, with suggestions for starting a prayer group. We found that the basic idea of the Experiment is that partners pray for thirty days, seeking answers to each other's problems. The guidelines suggested that newcomers start small by praying with a single partner. So Mike—who'd always been unwilling to pray aloud, even with me—asked Randy if he would pray with him. And I called up my minister's wife, Judy Schmidt, and asked her if she'd try the Experiment with me. Both agreed.

We began our prayer experiment in earnest. We knew, though, that we couldn't just pray and then sit, waiting for something to drop out of the blue. The cable TV job, for instance, was not going to improve; prayer helped Mike face that harsh fact. And so, though he had always hated job-hunting, he now attacked the want-ads with enthusiasm.

Thirty days went by and at that point Mike and Randy were so encouraged that they got some friends together and began a prayer group. If anybody had told me six months earlier that these rough-tough former cocktail-lounge musicians would be praying together, I would have laughed. But there they were, with bowed heads, talking to God about one another's hurts and needs.

A week after starting his prayer group, Mike was called in for an interview with a top national insurance company. The job was just what he had been hoping for.

While Mike waited for an offer, he was optimistic and full of faith. But I was more anxious and frightened than ever. Despite the fact that Judy and I were praying together, I was calling her two and three times a day, trying to cope with my feelings, because *I* was the one facing the bill collectors; *I* was the one wrestling with a tight budget, trying to feed our family on next to nothing, caring for Heidi and running our home.

I began to think: *We wives bear burdens with our men, and we encourage them. But who helps us bear our own burdens, who encourages us? Where do we get support?* Suddenly an all-too-obvious idea popped into my head: *Why not start a prayer group for wives?*

I asked Mike what he thought about my forming a group. "Sure," he replied. "You can do it, Claire." But then I hesitated, asking myself, *Am I really capable?* I've had a high-frequency hearing loss since birth, and I often rely on lip-reading. Because of this, when I become nervous, my speech tends to get garbled. My previously strong faith was wavering at this point, so how could I hope to lead a prayer group?

"Mike, suppose I make a mistake, forget what to say?"

"So what? Wing it." He wasn't letting me off the hook.

"I'm not a leader," I protested.

"Honey, we salesmen have a saying: 'You have nothing to lose and everything to gain, so pick up the phone and dial.' "

So that's what I did. I knew Judy would join the group. Who else? Linda Webber was a minister's daughter ... she wouldn't think I was a religious fanatic.

Linda was supportive. Even though she had three part-time jobs and a young son, she found the time to give the group a try. With two positive responses, I got the courage to dial seven more numbers. One more person accepted.

I read and reread the National Experiment guidelines until I had memorized them. The first meeting of our women's prayer group was held at our home. There were four of us: three Protestants and a Catholic. I opened with a short—a very short—prayer, asking God to be with us. My voice had a wobble I hoped wasn't too noticeable. Then, silence. I took a deep breath.

"Judy and I have been praying for more than thirty days now," I began. "We feel a need to support each other. Now, with this group, we believe we all can help one another by talking and praying about what is bothering us in our lives. Please don't feel you have to contribute if it makes you uncomfortable. But I'll tell you what's happened in my life ..."

Then, as simply as I could, I told my friends for the first time of the terrible pressures Mike and I had been facing.

"But you know," I said, "Judy and I have kept a log. At the beginning of our Thirty-Day Experiment, it was filled with negative thoughts. Toward the end, most of our entries were positive. I feel better about things, and I think Judy does too.

"The concept in the National Experiment guidelines that encouraged me to create a women's group is this: *God will accept you at any level of faith or doubt.* If He can believe that self-conscious, sometimes tongue-tied Claire Donch can accomplish something, then I can believe it too! Think about it."

One of the other women spoke up. "Well, I'm not much good at praying aloud, but I need help. My husband is underemployed ... just like Mike. And I'm having an awful time handling our three kids ... You know, my oldest, Joey, is only three. I need more patience ..." She stopped, suddenly embarrassed. Judy patted her hand in encouragement.

The other women began to open up about the things that were troubling them. Judy admitted she and her husband were having financial problems involving the sale of their home in New York City. Without the proceeds from a sale, they struggled to meet their current bills. She asked for prayer.

All at once I realized I had forgotten to be afraid! Instead, there was a beautiful feeling of caring in the room. And something even more wonderful—the presence of the Lord. He was there with us as we talked and prayed. The words of St. Paul came to me: "Bear ye one another's burdens, and so fulfil the law of Christ" (Galatians 6:2). And that "law" is simply to love one another. That was what we were doing. And that was why we felt Him there with us!

Before we closed with the Lord's Prayer, we agreed to pray for one another every day.

We decided to hold weekly meetings—and almost immediately we ran into problems with the husbands. Our meeting was scheduled at 8:00 P.M., just when one of the fellows was expecting his dinner. Another husband didn't fancy being a baby sitter. But eventually we worked our problems out and have stuck to our schedule.

Since we began last spring, our women's prayer group has gained some new members; others have dropped out. We're a small group; we think the Lord wants it that way until we're a little more experienced.

All of us have financial and related problems. One new member works part time to help make ends meet. Her particular problem is that her husband has had to take a job in a distant city. Like many of us, she had taken on chores ordinarily done by her husband—having the car serviced and mowing the lawn. When her husband comes home weekends, she tries to avoid burdening him with problems, so she finds the support of the group indispensible. However, she has been concerned about managing her time better. She has asked the group to pray about it.

So it goes, week by week. When one set of problems is resolved, there are always new ones to share and pray over.

Why has our women's group thrived? I think it's because we're "other-directed." When you stop to think of it, married women with children to raise can become isolated and self-absorbed. We get caught up in our own family's problems; we're starved for interaction with other adults.

So the prayer group gets us out of the house and out of ourselves. We realize in a deep way that we are *not* alone in our problems. Not all of us can attend every meeting. Sometimes there are only two of us. But it doesn't matter. Jesus Himself said: "For where two or three are gathered together in my name, there am I in the midst of them" (Matthew 18:20).

And what about my husband and me? Well, before we joined the National Experiment Mike and I were, in a sense, leading separate spiritual lives. Now we're closer than ever. We have a new respect for each other's beliefs. We concentrate on our unity in Christ, not on the differences. And, oh yes, Mike *was* offered a job by the insurance company; he accepted and is now happier in his work.

Are you facing problems? Are you scared, unsure? You *can't* be more afraid than this scaredy-cat was! And if I could step out in faith, anyone can. Let me tell you—prayer works. It works wonders. But you may never know, if you don't try it.

Akron at 8:00 A.M.

WILLIAM DEERFIELD

It was snowing when I arrived in Akron, Ohio, on the Friday evening before Thanksgiving of 1987. The TV news predicted twelve inches before morning. Besides the annoyance of snow, I wasn't looking forward to my assignment; there was a good possibility I'd fail to get a story.

Before I left New York City my editor said, "Get me the answer to this: What's the purpose of prayer breakfasts? Are they just pleasant get-togethers where church people meet other church people and pray, or do they accomplish something else?"

Ron Glosser, president of the National City Bank of Akron, and chairman and one of the organizers of the breakfast I was to attend the next morning, met me at the airport. As we drove to dinner, he assured me the breakfast would go on as scheduled, at 8:00 A.M. Saturday.

Good luck, I couldn't help thinking, as the car crept along through a descending curtain of white. How many of those invited would leave a warm bed early on a snowy Saturday morning for a "worthy cause" event like this?

After dinner, as we trudged through the snow, Ron and his wife, Lily, insisted I cancel my hotel reservations and stay at their home. An hour later, sitting at the counter in Ron and Lily's cozy kitchen sipping coffee, I asked Ron how the prayer breakfast came about.

"It started," he replied, "when Pete Geiger, who's a writer for the Akron *Beacon Journal,* gave me a copy of Wayne Alderson's biography, *Stronger Than Steel,* by R. C. Sproul (San Francisco: Harper & Row, 1983). Alderson is the founder of Value of the Person Consultants, an organization that holds seminars nationwide to help bring about reconciliation between labor and management by using the Judeo-Christian ethic of respect and concern for each individual person. The seminars point out, for instance, that contract negotiations often break down because both management and the union become so rigid in defense of each's own viewpoint that they reach a bitter impasse.

"Reading Wayne's book," Ron continued, "I realized he had the same concerns I had in my attempt to help solve our economic and labor-management problems here in Akron, especially in the areas of contract negotiations and unemployment due to our declining industries here.

"At our church, when I suggested we have a labor-management prayer breakfast to get the 'Value of the Person' message out to the public, somebody objected that including *labor-management* in the title would be too 'divisive.' But our minister, Knute Larson, agreed with me that our focus would bring labor-management problems into a spiritual context. 'It's something that needs prayer,' he said.

" 'You mean, we'll actually *pray* at this thing?' somebody quipped.

" 'Yes,' Knute replied. 'We'll pray, have special music, speakers. The breakfast will be a symbol—a rallying point from which real change can begin.'

"So," Ron concluded, "after that, a lot of work had to be done to get a large representation of both labor and management to attend."

The next morning, the snow had stopped. Ron left early to help with arrangements. Later, Lily Glosser and I slipped and slid toward town in her car.

The breakfast was being held at the Tangier, the largest meeting hall in Akron. When we entered, the place was jammed in spite of the weather. I was thinking about what Ron had said about the economic situation in the Akron area. As if reading my thoughts, Lily said, "People are desperate for answers."

A few minutes later I was introduced to Tom Edminston, a Teamsters truck driver, from Local 24 in Akron. "Do you think a labor-management prayer breakfast like this is valuable, Tom?" I asked.

"Well," he said, eying my tape recorder, "if it's just for show, then we might as well stay home. As for the labor-management part," he continued with a rueful laugh, "boy ... I'll tell ya ... there needs to be a lot more prayer breakfasts between the two. Frankly, I'm antagonistic toward companies. Three years ago the firm I worked for pulled out of Akron." He also seemed bitter because he felt his union hadn't done enough to encourage his company to stay in Akron.

Just then Ron Glosser called the guests to order. Before Edminston disappeared into the crowd, he agreed to give me his reactions after the breakfast.

The program opened with an invocation by Rev. Ronald Fowler, of Arlington (Ohio) Church of God, urging serious "contemplation of God's will" in the proceedings. Next, a gospel group called Divine Hope sang a hymn stressing the need for repentance. Then there were more prayers. Rev. Knute Larson, pastor of The Chapel, echoed the message of repentance. Referring to the hostility and bitterness that is sometimes present in the workplace, he asked God to forgive those who were guilty of this and to help all to learn to love one another. He concluded by challenging the guests to "pray for someone at work you don't like." Dr. William Muse, president of the University of Akron, offered "thoughts in the form of a prayer" on the need for better labor-management relations. A prayer of thanksgiving was given by Dr. Gordon Werkema, president of Malone College, who thanked God for "the opportunity and challenge to take seriously Your command to love our neighbors as ourselves."

After the prayers, there were "greetings" from local leaders of labor and management, including Ken Coss, international secretary-treasurer of the United Rubber Workers union, and County Executive John Morgan. Morgan told the guests that he had attended a Value of the

Person seminar and he thought that "seeds have been planted."

Finally Wayne Alderson, the main speaker, was introduced. A tall, rangy man who looks like a cross between a coal miner and a cowboy, Alderson got right to the point: "In this country, I do not see 'labor-management relations.' I see a *lack* of labor-management relations."

He spoke of his father, a miner who fought all his life for the dignity of workers. Then he talked of his own forty-three years of struggle to bring about reconciliation in the workplace. "I stand before you," he boomed, "as someone who's had a *bellyful* of conflict in business and industry, of people saying that confrontation is the only way."

Alderson said he was convinced that such an attitude on the part of unions and management bordered on stupidity. He said that everyone—workers and managers alike—need to be respected and valued.

"When you leave here today," he concluded, "you have a choice: You can continue to do it in the human way of confrontation, of alienation. Or there's another choice—God's way: reconciliation, love, respect for others. The question you have to ask is not 'Can we bring about reconciliation?' A deeper question you have to ask yourself this morning is: 'Will I personally work toward reconciliation?' Think about it: *You* can make a difference where you are."

The applause was thunderous.

Then, after a brief time for discussion at our tables, the event closed with the five hundred guests standing and singing a rousing rendition of "How Great Thou Art." And their fervor made it not only a hymn but their own prayer of praise.

The comments after the breakfast were, without exception, enthusiastic and thoughtful. Dr. Werkema summed up the mood of many when he told me, "I had thirty-five guests here. I'm not sure all of them agree with the ideas expressed here, but they got something to think about—and to pray about."

Trying to get a viewpoint from labor, I looked around for Tom Edminston, the Teamsters driver I had talked to before the breakfast, but he apparently had already left the hall.

Something was still bothering me on my flight back to New York. People seemed to be challenged by the breakfast's speakers, but what about concrete results?

Thanksgiving and Christmas came and went. I made a stab at writing this piece, but it wasn't coming together. Then one morning I got a call from Ron Glosser, who had some exciting news. For the first time in memory, he said, two county unions had settled their contracts well before their December 31 deadline, and many people were giving the credit to the impact made by Wayne Alderson's seminars and the Labor-Management Prayer Breakfast.

So I placed a call to County Executive John Morgan. He confirmed what Glosser had told me. In the eight years he's been in office, Morgan said, both unions had prolonged strikes, and even when they didn't strike, contract negotiations always went down to the wire and beyond. But this time, he told me, Local 2696 of the American Federation of

State, County and Municipal Employees had agreed to a contract two weeks before the deadline, and Local 1229 settled a few days later.

Then I called Sharon MacBride, president of Local 2696. She told me that the seminars and the prayer breakfast had "definitely helped" in their union contract negotiations.

"When John invited me to the prayer breakfast," she said, "quite frankly I didn't want to go. But Wayne Alderson cut through all the garbage. He doesn't try to placate either labor or management. He makes comments that neither side wants to hear. Yet they have to accept it, because what he's saying is true.

"After the breakfast," she continued, "I went up to John Morgan and actually thanked him for inviting me. I told him that with the decline of the rubber industry in Akron and all, the breakfast was a start toward doing something."

I still wanted to get the reaction to the breakfast from Teamster driver Tom Edminston. He represented the rank-and-file worker, the most vulnerable—and most skeptical—part of the labor-management equation.

I wasn't able to reach him until late the next evening. "Frankly, I didn't know what to expect that morning," he said, "but the prayer breakfast convinced me of one thing: to stop hating. Since then I've prayed for my ex-employer and the union. And things are a lot better for me now. Don't get me wrong. I still want justice done, but I'm not out for blood anymore."

I had my story now. Many people had been inspired—

and changed—on that November morning; they had gone away from the breakfast determined to make a difference in their daily lives, on their jobs—plain ordinary workers, college presidents, union leaders, journalists, clergy, business managers.

Maybe, as my editor suspected, there are lots of different kinds of prayer breakfasts. But this one in Akron happened to focus on a real problem. As for his question, "What's the purpose of prayer breakfasts?", here in Akron I learned it was one more way to bring God where He should be—in this case right into the workplace.

The Four Days

RON ROSS

The baler *chunk-chunked* rhythmically behind me as I turned in the tractor seat to glance at our new neighbors walking past. Interesting-looking people, men with beads, women in long dresses.

Not that such things were unusual in Deer Island, Oregon, nowadays. Newcomers had begun moving here from Portland in the mid-70s. Nice enough folks, kind of kept to themselves. This latest group, for instance. When a bunch of them moved into the ramshackle apartment down the road, my wife went over with some homemade preserves. They seemed to appreciate it. Didn't ask her in, though. Didn't give their names.

Well, we sure didn't want to pry into anyone's business. Trouble was, some of the newcomers were doing things you couldn't help but notice. Two young couples who had come from Portland, for example, lived above and worked in the grocery store down at the crossroads next to an abandoned school and the church. Used to be you'd meet your neighbors there, stop and chat. Nowadays you couldn't hear a word over that booming rock music. You'd hand your money to the silent fellow behind the counter and get never a nod. His black hair went to his waist, and dark glasses hid his expression like a locked door.

Here in Oregon we don't like to think unkindly about people, but lately things had turned up missing from our toolsheds and barns. What concerned us most, though, was our young people. The grocery store had always been the place for kids to congregate; now it was even more so with the addition of a video-game arcade. Our kids were coming home with a whole new vocabulary.

"Daddy, what's a reefer?" "I think Tim acted sort of high in math class." The kids would laugh nervously as they unfolded bits of information around the security of the dining room table. Their mother and I found it difficult to talk even to one another about the changes taking place in our rural community.

The end of the row. I turned the tractor and, as so often before, tried to push the formless doubts from my mind. That very night down at church, however, they took on a shape and a name. I usually enjoyed these monthly deacons' meetings in the fireplace room. That night, though, Pastor Ray Anthony was frowning. "Friends," he said, "Deer Island has a drug problem."

He went on to report what was happening in the church's newly launched youth program. Attendance had been good, probably because there wasn't much else for teenagers to do. The program drew children from the "Portland people" too. From the beginning Ray had sensed something different about some of these youngsters. They joined in the discussion, but gave odd answers to some of his questions. Occasional hilarious laughter over nothing. A closer look confirmed his suspicions: dilated eyes, a tell-tale odor.

It was out in the open, the truth we'd all been aware of but hadn't wanted to confront. Now that Ray had broken the silence, each one of us had some bit of evidence to report. We were almost certain the two couples helping in the store were luring kids into drugs, first by giving, then by selling. For the most part it was not affecting the children of the congregation directly ... not yet. And meanwhile, what about our relationship to the young drug users—boys and girls coming to youth meetings right here in this fireplace room? They were in need of help.

Over the next few weeks we learned that the problem was worse than we'd suspected. Many of the newcomers, it turned out, were longtime addicts. One night the state police set up a road barricade and arrested a man and a woman practically in front of our farmhouse. We learned later that both had served time in jail for drug peddling.

The following month eight of us attended a meeting called by Pastor Ray to decide on a course of action. But what action? What chance had we, a small rural congregation, against a plague that baffled even the experts? What could we do that we hadn't been doing all along—calling on these folks, trying to be neighborly, inviting them to various church functions.

"For all the response," one woman deacon said, "I might as well talk to the fence posts." We belonged to different worlds. In such a situation, what could we do?

"We can pray," Pastor Ray told us.

Pray? Well, sure, we'd been doing that too, individually, off and on. But since nobody had any better suggestion, the eight of us bowed our heads.

For a while there was some twisting about on the hard metal seats in that fireplace room. As the minutes dragged by, I grew impatient. Where was this getting us? We needed action! This was a case for the state troopers, or a federal narcotics agency.

Gradually, though, the fidgeting ceased; over the small fireplace room settled a potent silence. A living silence: the hush of a deep communion.

Thirty minutes passed. I'd never prayed silently this long before—or felt so connected to other people and to God. At the end of a full hour, a thought stood out in my mind that surely had not originated there.

A fast.

A fast? Like in the Bible? Like in Jehoshaphat's time? Yes, I remembered. Judah was being attacked by three powerful armies, and King Jehoshaphat proclaimed a fast for everyone. In the end, the attacking armies killed off one another, and Judah didn't even have to fight.

I looked up. Pastor Ray was standing. "It will be a four-day fast, then," he concluded for all the world as though there had been a discussion about it. I nodded wonderingly. How could this be? How could eight people reach a decision without a word being uttered?

Unless ... unless in the silence God had spoken. And if God had spoken—then He was taking on our battle, as He'd taken on Jehoshaphat's! Starting now, Tuesday night, we agreed, the eight of us would embark on four days of concentrated prayer and fasting. This would be a brand-new experience for most of us, but there was a hopeful excitement buzzing through the room as we dismissed that evening. Our united request: that God would either bring these people to Himself, or move them out. As one man put it, "Move hearts or move bodies!"

The first day of the fast was pretty challenging for me, a part-time farmer and paper-mill worker who is fairly slim. I wondered if I would have the energy to finish the harvest. But I'd set my jaw and fix my mind on that prayer. I knew it had to be even harder for the women in our group, who were continuing to prepare heaps of fried chicken and biscuits for their large families.

The eight of us met nightly in the fireplace room for prayer and encouragement. And after that first day none of us felt hungry. What was more, our prayer-fueled hopefulness seemed to be mounting.

The four-day fast ended at midnight on Saturday. The next day, Sunday, we couldn't see any effect on the community; we reminded ourselves it was too soon to expect results. But neither was there any sign of change all that following week. In the grocery store the "Portland people" continued to look past us as though we didn't exist.

By the time my family and I took our places in church that second Sunday I was feeling pretty crestfallen—and a little ashamed of myself. What had got into me? I had been half expecting that some prayers and skipping a few meals could affect deep-seated patterns of addiction and lifestyle in people who were scarcely aware of our existence.

Beside me in the pew the kids were twisting around, staring toward the back of the church. I turned to look—and saw him, sitting just inside the door. Waist-length black hair; dark, emotion-absent eyes: the man from the grocery store. Quickly I faced front. "Don't stare!" I whispered.

At the close of the service, I hurried to the rear of the church. But the man departed without a word of response to our greetings at the door. We "fasters" glanced anxiously at one another.

On the third Sunday, the man was back, this time with his wife and children. And they all went forward at the altar call! This family began bringing other families, reaching out to them as we had not known how to, "turning them on to Jesus," as they themselves put it. Many of those on drugs, we learned, had been miserable in that lifestyle. The excitement with which they passed on their newfound freedom to others was like something out of the Book of Acts. It wasn't unusual for a new convert to point across the now-crowded sanctuary: "Please pray for Jim and Polly over there. They need to know Jesus Christ." We more conventional churchgoers would cringe at these declarations, but offense was never taken—and often as not, Jim and Polly would indeed come to Christ! Users brought drug paraphernalia to Pastor Ray: "Please destroy these."

By now all eight of us were ashamed of asking God to "move hearts or move bodies." Watching how marvelously He could change hearts, we felt we'd been wrong to want Him to remove the others from our neighborhood. Moving bodies was no solution; it simply changed the locale of the problem—perhaps to an area where no one was praying.

One bright Sunday morning, however, three months after that four-day fast, we were chatting in the church vestibule at the close of the service. The crowd of faces included one of the families from the store, smiling regulars now.

Suddenly Pastor Ray looked down the street and pointed. There, behind the grocery store, a truck was being loaded with furniture. The other couple, who'd persisted in their way of life, were moving away.

Without a word, our little group of eight filed into the fireplace room to give thanks to God for honoring our prayer, however deficient. We didn't know how He'd done it—whether through earthly means or heavenly ones. We only knew from the moment we "set ourselves to seek the Lord," we were like Jehoshaphat: The battle was not ours, but God's.

Because it *is* a battle. Not, ultimately, against drug smugglers or organized crime or any other human agency. This is a spiritual assault and our most effective weapons are spiritual ones. I'm not a theologian, and I don't understand what happens when people start praying. But if prayer changed things here, maybe it can change things in other places.

Here in Deer Island, His orders to us were to fast. In another place He may have a different plan. But that He does have a strategy, a divine one shaped in invisible realms, we have never doubted since the night we grew quiet and asked.

Prevailing Prayer

Lord, what a change within us one short hour
Spent in Thy presence would prevail to make!
What heavy burdens from our bosoms take!
What parched grounds refresh as with a shower!
We kneel, and all around us seems to lower;
We rise, and all, the distant and the near,
Stands forth in sunny outline, brave and clear;
We kneel, how weak! we rise, how full of power!
Why, therefore, should we do ourselves this wrong,
Or others—that we are not always strong—
That we are sometimes overborne with care—
That we should ever weak or heartless be,
Anxious or troubled—when with us is prayer,
And joy and strength and courage are with Thee?

RICHARD CHEVENIX TRENCH (1807–1886)

PRAYING FOR OTHERS

Our Father ...

You cannot say the Lord's Prayer
And even once say "I."
You cannot say the Lord's Prayer
And even once say "My."
Nor can you pray the Lord's Prayer
And not pray for one another,
For when you ask for daily bread,
You must include your brother,
For others are included in each and every plea;
From beginning to the end of it,
It does not once say "Me."

AUTHOR UNKNOWN

How to Feel Useful

CORA VIRGINIA PERRY

Last year I was hospitalized with a severe case of pneumonia. Since I was sixty-five and lived alone, I was transferred to a nursing home for the recuperation period. I was very weak and needed help with everything, even to turn over or sit up in bed. It was very discouraging.

One day, feeling utterly helpless, I complained to the nurse. "Why do I keep on living? What good am I? I'm just a nuisance. I can't do anything for anyone."

"Oh, I don't know about that, Miss Perry," she answered with a smile. "I think there is something you can do. You can pray for others."

What good medicine that was! There, flat on my back, I began to pray for my fellow patients, for the doctors and nurses, for world leaders, for anyone who came to mind. And as I did, I found I was moping less, and focusing more on the world outside. Without knowing it, I was getting out of myself, out into the world—if only in spirit. And eventually I was there physically too!

Today I'm living at home, and I'm able to take care of myself, but I'm still following that excellent prescription for feeling useful!

What Praying for Others Can Do for You

NORMAN VINCENT PEALE

Not long ago I had a vivid reminder of the power that can be generated when we pray—really pray—for others.

I happened to wake up at 3:00 A.M. on a Sunday morning. I had gone to bed early as I always do on a Saturday night when I have to preach the next day, but here I was, all of a sudden, wide awake. I tried every known device to go back to sleep. I counted sheep, I said the 23rd Psalm half a dozen times. But still I could not go back to sleep. Finally I got up at four o'clock, went into my library, and picked up one book and magazine after another. Nothing held my interest.

Some years ago in Switzerland, I purchased a large and beautiful eagle carved from a single block of wood, and brought it back to my library. Made by one of the old-time Swiss wood-carvers, it is really a work of art. The eagle has his wings spread and is taking off from some high eminence. I sat looking at the eagle, remembering when I bought it and the old man who made it, and then, naturally, I began to say aloud a passage of Scripture: "... they shall mount up with wings as eagles; they shall run, and not be weary; and they shall walk, and not faint" (Isaiah 40:31).

This in turn led to a thought about a friend, a pastor who says that occasionally, when he needs spiritual help, he goes into the church and walks the aisles. He places his hand on the pew where a certain person sits each Sunday and prays for that person by name. And he repeats the process at various pews in the empty church. The pastor says that this procedure always brings great blessing to him as well as to the persons he prays for. So, motivated by my friend's example, there alone in the early morning, I started to visualize everyone I should pray for.

The first person was my wife Ruth. Then I prayed for our three children and their spouses, then for our eight grandchildren. I prayed for all the relatives I could call to mind. Then my mind went to the church, and I prayed for the other ministers. I prayed for all the secretaries. Then one by one I prayed for all the elders and all the deacons. Finally I began to visualize the congregation at the church and prayed for everyone I could think of by name. Then I prayed for the doormen in our apartment house and for all the people with whom I am associated in any way.

Actually, I must have prayed for five hundred people by name. By this time it was 6:00 A.M. All of a sudden I felt better than I had felt in a long time. I was full of energy, and boundless enthusiasm surged within me. I wouldn't have gone back to sleep for anything. I was ravenously hungry and went and awakened my wife.

"Get up! It's six A.M.," I said. "I'm hungry, and let us have no piddling breakfast. I want bacon and eggs, the whole works!" And I ate a man-sized breakfast.

I went to the church and delivered a sermon and shook hands with hundreds of people. Then I went to a luncheon and gave a talk, and on to an afternoon engagement, and at eleven o'clock that night I was still going strong. I was not even tired! Such an excess of energy was mine as to astound me, and with it came a tremendous new feeling of love for life.

Now, I'm not psychologist enough to explain exactly what happened. I guess I got outside myself. Consciously, even subconsciously, I completely forgot myself in loving all those other people and praying for them and taking their burdens on myself. But this didn't add any weight, either. It added wings! And it left me happy and joyous, revitalized, reborn. Actually, I rose up "with wings as eagles."

So now, whenever I feel enervated or depressed, I repeat that prayer process. And I offer this experience as a suggestion of how you, too, may not only help others by prayer but also find marvelous new life for yourself.

The Navy Yard Secret

ANN ROOT

Some years ago my brother Burton held a job as a carpenter at the Philadelphia Navy Yard. His boss there liked his work, but one thing bothered Burton. The men swore all the time and, on the lunch hour, drank and made fun of Burton who, because of his Quaker beliefs, did not join in.

During the silent meditation period at Quaker meeting on Sunday, he asked God for guidance. We Quakers are taught to rely on Jesus' promise that "where two or three are gathered together in my name, there am I in the midst of them" (Matthew 18:20). And so we shut our eyes, relax, and listen; but first we usually say, "Father, I thank Thee that Thou hearest me always," and then we ask for what we need, just as we would ask another person. Burton told me later that he had asked God what to do about this problem at work—the drinking and the swearing—and these words immediately came to him: "God bless you and wake you up."

He took this to be the answer to his prayer; and so, to the first man that swore, Burton silently said, "God bless you and wake you up." Almost instantly the man stopped swearing. Later, as Burton repeated these words when other men swore or drank, they immediately stopped. Burton did not tell the men or the boss of his prayer, not even when he was transferred to another section and the boss told him how pleased he was, how the men liked Burton and what a good influence he had been. The secret was between Burton and God.

Knowing how this prayer worked for Burton, I have for years used it daily myself. I say it silently to everyone I meet. Although I never know how it affects anyone else's life, I know it helps me.

Instead of being critical or finding fault with people, holding them up to God for a moment in silence with a *God bless you and wake you up* keeps both the pray-er and the one prayed for in God's presence.

A Mighty Fortress

ROBERT J. "MUTT" OSBORNE

When I was an aerial gunner on a B-17 bomber flying out of England in 1943, we seldom came back from a raid over Germany or Occupied Europe without extensive damage to our Flying Fortress caused by German fighters or antiaircraft fire. That deadly hail of machine-gun bullets and shrapnel caused numerous casualties among crew members too. I remember we talked a lot about defensive armor, and wished we had some. Later on flak jackets were issued and did save some lives. But the most effective shield that ever surrounded me had nothing to do with armor-plated seats or bulletproof jackets. It was manufactured a long way from those furious combats in the sky. But without it I wouldn't be here today.

Let me tell you a little about myself. I was born in the low country of South Carolina, grew up on the hill of Puddin Swamp in the Turbeville community. Our family had a two-horse farm (took two mules to work it), but we lost it in the

Great Depression when just about everybody went broke. My daddy had to fall back on sharecropping, and things were awfully tight. Nobody had any money; everything was barter, and there wasn't much to barter. We boys had to fish and hunt to keep eating. I remember being given the old shotgun and one shell—all we could afford—and told to come back with one squirrel or else face big trouble. When we went rabbit hunting we didn't take a gun at all, just a pocketful of those heavy square nuts that hold a wheel on the axle of a wagon. We threw those, and we got so we didn't miss very often.

My daddy wasn't much for religion, but my mother was. Everyone called her Miss Martha, and she used to say she was going to teach us young 'uns right from wrong if she had to beat it in with a stick. We went barefoot all week, and often shirtless too, but Miss Martha would round up all the neighborhood kids on Sunday and see that we wore shoes and went to Sunday school in the old Methodist church down at Turbeville. When the war came, she got all the church mothers who had boys in the service to meet every day and pray for our safety.

Because I weighed only about one hundred thirty pounds, my nickname was Mutt, after the smaller character in the famous comic strip *Mutt and Jeff.* When I graduated from aerial gunnery school, my size made me a natural candidate for ball-turret gunner. The ball turret, on the underside of a Fortress, was so small that the gunner couldn't even wear a parachute. You were down there with two .50-caliber machine guns and nothing else.

Some air crews were lucky. I can't say that ours was. On our very first mission we were shot up so badly that we crash-landed on the English coast. That was the end of our Fortress named *Little Chuck.* We got another named *The Last Chance,* and it almost was. On one mission, after we were hit hard, the bombardier and navigator decided to bail out. The bombardier pulled his ripcord too soon. The billowing silk streamed through the escape hatch and then pinned him against the opening so he couldn't move. He was just about being flogged to death. The wildly flapping chute came and tangled itself around my guns; I couldn't see or do anything. I had to go up into the plane, cut the bombardier out of his harness and pull him back aboard. I got a nasty slash across my hand from my own knife, but finally somehow we got back to England.

Early in November we were ordered to bomb Gelsenkirchen, a German industrial center in the Ruhr. It was my twentieth mission and it would be tough. I wasn't flying with my regular crew; I was a substitute gunner on another airplane.

We made it to the target and dropped our bombs, but then it seemed to me that the German fighters—Me 109s and Fw 190s—came in like a swarm of bees. I could feel our plane shudder from multiple hits, and when I swung my turret around to look at the engines, I saw that two of them were out. That meant we would be losing altitude and dropping behind the formation, a sitting duck for more fighter attacks.

I didn't hear any order to bail out (actually our communications system was destroyed), but looking down I saw parachutes begin to blossom under our plane. I counted eight of them. There were ten of us in the crew. German fighters were still coming in, but I figured if everyone was leaving I had better leave too. So I crawled up into the body of the Fortress and clipped on my chute, which I always kept right beside the turret.

The bomb-bay doors were still open, and I was about to jump when I happened to look ahead and saw the pilot slumped over in the space between his seat and the co-pilot's. It seemed to me that he moved a little bit, which meant he wasn't dead. For a moment I hesitated, torn between the desire to jump and save myself, and reluctance to leave a wounded man to what would be certain death. I guess my mother's lessons about right and wrong had been hammered in more firmly than I knew. I was frightened almost out of my senses, but I found myself walking along the catwalk above the bomb bay until I came to the pilot. He had been hit in the head either by flak or by machine-gun bullets and was barely conscious. The copilot had left the plane on automatic pilot; we were still flying on only two engines.

I knelt beside the wounded pilot, scared stiff and wondering what to do. I looked through the windshield to see if the formation was leaving us (it was), and as I did I saw something totally incredible. Reflected in the glass was a picture—a vivid picture—of a group of women gathered around a large dining-room table, praying. I knew who they were, because in almost every letter my mother told me she and her friends were praying. Even stranger, standing behind those women were their sons in uniform. I knew them too, and I also knew that some of them were dead, killed in action.

As I stared in amazement, the picture faded, but I heard—or seemed to hear—a commanding voice that spoke three words: "Take it back!" I knew it could not be the pilot, who was mumbling incoherently. I knew too that I was being ordered to take charge of our crippled airplane and fly it back to Britain.

But how could I? On practice missions I sometimes had been allowed to sit in the copilot's seat and "fly" the aircraft. But this "stick time" was insignificant. I had never attempted to land or take off in a four-engined bomber, much less one with two engines out. But the voice came again, clear and authoritative: "Take it back."

Now I seemed to be aware of a figure standing behind me. I thought for a moment the tail gunner had left his position and come forward. But that was impossible because I had seen eight chutes. There could only be two of us left in the plane: the pilot and me. But again the voice spoke, and this time it gave me the compass heading for England. I think it was 322 degrees.

My reaction to all this, to the picture of the praying women, to the resonant voice, to the inexplicable presence of a third man, was a kind of total acceptance. My rational mind couldn't believe any of it, but I accepted it. I felt as if a strong, wise commander was giving me orders. It was my job to obey them, and I felt the terrible sense of panic and helplessness begin to subside.

I crawled into the copilot's seat, took the Fortress off automatic pilot, and swung it around to the heading I had been given. I still felt the presence of the third man behind me, but I didn't look around. The formation had gone ahead without us. Off to the left at about eleven o'clock I saw a squadron of German fighters queuing up to let us have it. We were helpless and they knew it.

Then suddenly, right ahead of us, was a towering cumulus cloud. By rights that cloud wasn't supposed to be there; it wasn't on our weather charts. But there it was, and we ducked into it like a hunted deer. Visibility dropped to zero. No fighters could find us in such cover. We flew along steadily, our two good engines pulling us, and when we finally came out of the clouds at about ten thousand feet, we were over the North Sea, and the coastline of England lay ahead of us. A tremendous sense of relief surged through me, and I glanced once over my shoulder. Was that figure still standing behind me?

No one was there.

But we still weren't home. When we crossed the coast I began looking for a place to try to land. I had no idea how to find our own base, the 381st Bomb Group, but finally I saw a runway with some transports on it. When I tried to talk to the tower, I didn't know the proper call signs to identify myself, and they kept telling me not to land. The Germans had been known to load a captured Fortress with explosives and send it over England with very little gas, hoping that when it came down it would blow up something. The radio operators in the tower were women, and I couldn't understand their British accents, just one emphatic word, "No! No! No!" I guess they couldn't comprehend my Carolina country talk very well either, but I hoped they would figure it was something no German pilot could possibly imitate. In any case, I had to land, because I was running out of fuel; red lights were showing on all the gauges. I told the tower I would circle once and then I was coming in. I asked them to have the crash wagon and the ambulances ready. Then I swung my big crippled bird in a wide circle and headed for the runway.

I was flying on only two engines, and the bomb-bay doors were creating a lot of drag, so I was moving at only eighty or ninety miles per hour. I didn't put the wheels down because I wasn't sure how to do it, and anyway I figured it might be safer with the wheels up. So I just eased her in, holding the nose up and letting the tail kind of sag. When I cut the power, the tail hit first, and then we skidded along on the belly of the plane, smooth as glass, almost to the end of the runway, where we just slewed around and stopped.

I got out of my window and went around and pulled the pilot out of his window. I put him on my shoulders and walked to the edge of the wing and jumped off; it wasn't very far to the ground. I was a little afraid of fire, but I knew we had almost no gas left, so I wasn't too worried. I dragged the pilot about fifty feet and fell down beside him just as an ambulance came screeching up. They wanted to put me on a stretcher, but I told them to take the pilot first. "He's wounded," I said. "I'm not." By now they were spraying the airplane with foam for fire prevention. Someone said to me, "Are there any more men on board?" I said, "I don't think you'll find any." Then a wave of blackness descended and I passed out.

When I woke up in the hospital, they fed me some broth and said I was suffering from total exhaustion. I couldn't quarrel with that. The pilot was badly hurt; he lingered a few days and then died. Before he died he signed a letter to our base commander recommending me for a Congressional Medal of Honor. They didn't give me that, but they did award me a Silver Star. And a long leave in London.

When I tried to tell our intelligence officers about the third man who had been on the plane, they smiled indulgently and said something about "understandable hallucinations."

I can understand their doubts, but I have no doubts of my own. I know it was our Lord Jesus Christ who came to me when I was in terrible danger and told me what to do and helped me do it. I believe too that prayer put an invisible shield around me that day over the flaming skies over Nazi Germany. It can guard you too, if someone will just pray for you as fervently as that little group of women prayed for me. So many years ago. In a quiet rural community. On the hill of Puddin Swamp.

I Am Living, Breathing Proof

SANDRA SIMPSON LESOURD

In the living room of a cozy ranch house nestled next to the rimrock cliffs that border Billings, Montana, a group of women sat with clasped hands and bowed heads. "Dear Lord," Marlene said. "We're here to pray for Sandy. She's in deep trouble. She doesn't know we are praying for her, but Lord, we ask humbly that You be with her and strengthen her."

At that same moment, in the summer of 1978, I sat in Warm Springs, Montana, staring through the grime-streaked windows of the State Hospital for Mental Disorders. My weight was over two hundred pounds, my skin was gray and my hair greasy—a sad situation for someone who in 1956 had represented her home state of Vermont at the Miss America Pageant in Atlantic City.

How had I got myself into such a miserable condition? There's a lot of scientific jargon to describe compulsive personalities like mine. My motto since my teen years had been: Anything worth doing is worth *over*doing. I would tell people, "When my motor is running, I can't seem to shut it off."

And eventually my compulsive *over*doing resulted in debilitating addictions to everything from alcohol, prescription drugs and nicotine, to overeating and out-of-control shopping sprees.

"It's time to start," said Marlene. They were meeting again as they did every Thursday morning, these ten or twelve women from the First United Methodist Church in Billings. After opening with songs of praise, there were prayers of thanksgiving—and then progress reports about the people they'd been praying for. The meetings generally lasted about two hours, each woman bringing a notebook to record the prayers they'd be making throughout the week. Special prayer attention was focused on the group's "Ten-Most-Wanted List," a list they had compiled, containing desperate cases of people most in need of the Lord: a teenager on drugs, a mother with Alzheimer's, a husband in the last stages of cancer, and a recent "most wanted" addition—Sandy.

So many people had tried unsuccessfully to help me: my family, friends, counselors and psychiatrists, including those at a treatment center where I'd spent a month. I put my head in my hands. It seemed hopeless. Could I ever go home? Would I ever be whole again?

Since the group believed in the power released by affirming the best in the person being prayed for, over and over they inserted Sandy's name into Scripture verses: "Strength and dignity are [*Sandy's*] *clothing. ...* [*Sandy*] *opens her mouth with wisdom, and the teaching of kindness is on her tongue. ... Her children rise up and call her blessed" (Proverbs 31:25, 26, 28,* RSV*).*

And then the women asked God "to transform Sandy, send Your emissaries across her path to witness to her, to free her from bondage."

I *was* in bondage—to a suicidal depression and spiritual darkness. Every time I closed my eyes, an inky black curtain fell across my conscious mind, and I was unable to summon any positive or pleasing visual images. It was terrifying to be lying in bed with my eyes closed and see nothing but forbidding night—or worse, evil, mocking faces.

One day a young woman named Karen entered the hospital and was assigned to a room adjacent to mine. Her fiancé, it was reported, had been killed in an accident. Karen was inconsolable. Over and over she kept crying out, "Help me, Jesus! Help me, Jesus!"

Karen's constant yelling was aggravating. And the worst thing was, she attached herself to me. I tried to avoid Karen, but she followed me, her dark brown eyes pleading for me to help her.

Then, on a sultry July night, I was tossing restlessly in my hospital bed, when I sensed a presence. I sat up. Karen was standing in the doorway, her white robe startlingly bright in the moonlight.

She approached my bed, crying softly. "Oh, Sandy, does Jesus love me? Does Jesus really love me?" I could tell from her pleading voice that this was the only thing in the world that mattered to her.

What to do? What to say? I longed to comfort this weeping young woman but felt incapable of reassuring anybody of anything. Yet I had to do something. Taking Karen in my arms, I stroked her damp hair. It had been a long time since I'd held anyone or offered comfort—I'd always been the one *demanding* it.

I cleared my throat awkwardly. "Yes, Karen," I said. "Jesus—"

I stopped in astonishment. My heart was beating furiously, I felt warm and cold at the same time. What was I saying to this young woman? Why were these words having such power over her—and over *me?* "Karen," I said. "Jesus loves you. He *really* does."

Her sobbing stopped in an instant. She wiped her eyes with the back of her hand, thanked me in a voice of childlike gratitude, and slipped out of my room and back to hers.

I lay back down, puzzled at the strange lightness, almost giddiness, that I was feeling. The room seemed filled with a fragrant coolness.

"[Sandy] opens her mouth with wisdom, and the teaching of kindness is on her tongue. ... Her children rise up and call her blessed."

Thursday morning. The intercessors were meeting. "Dear Lord," Naomi said, leading the others in prayer, "God did not give [Sandy] a spirit of timidity but a spirit of power and love and self-control" (2 Timothy 1:7, RSV*). "And with his stripes [Sandy is] healed"* (*Isaiah 53:5,* RSV).

A few days after Karen's nighttime visit to my room, she left the hospital just as suddenly as she had arrived. I puzzled about what had happened between us; for the first time in my long illness—and almost against my will—I seemed to have helped another person.

Was there something different happening to me? A glimmer of joy here, a flicker of wonder there? I'd been noticing the birds outside my window, a rose in a vase in the patients' lounge, the picture of a child in the recreation area.

I stared out the window into a small grassy courtyard. The morning sun had appeared over the building annex, casting shadows from a slatted roof overhang into my room. Across my skirt and onto the floor fell a pattern of stripes. Out of nowhere, words came into my mind: *And with his stripes we are healed.*

They sounded scriptural, but what did I know about the Bible? Could I have heard these words as a child in Sunday school? Strange, yet the words were strongly, deeply reassuring. Was it possible that I could get better after all?

Marge, Loretta, Eva, Dottie, Betty, Bess—the prayer witnesses were faithful to their tasks. Many of them prayed not only on Thursdays but on every day of the week too, sometimes aloud during morning and evening devotions, sometimes silently while waiting in line at checkout counters or sitting in traffic. Again and again their prayers went out: "[Sandy] can do all things in Him who strengthens [her]" (Philippians 4:13, RSV).

To everyone's surprise, including my own, I was making such good progress that for the first time, the hospital staff felt I might make it on my own. A visit home was in order.

The first morning back in Billings in my own bed, I awoke terrified. How could I make up to my family for all my irresponsible behavior over the past fifteen years? Feelings of guilt and fear overwhelmed me. *Sleep in,* came the tempting voice inside my head. *Stay right here in bed.* That was the way I had handled things in the past.

But a new voice inside me spoke. *Get up and get going. Now!*

The old ways were entrenched, though, resistant to something new. I was afraid. No, I'd stay in bed today and start my new life tomorrow.

Get up. Do it now! The voice wouldn't stop—and I actually started to think I might *enjoy* getting on with my life. I got up, showered, put in a load of wash, made an appointment to have my hair cut and mopped the kitchen floor.

Major victories! As I moved from task to task, I was aided by a new inner feeling, a positive inner reinforcement that could be gentle and encouraging but at the same time insistent and strong. In the past my inner voice had always been negative, undermining and relentlessly critical. Now I felt a resolve and new sense of purpose that shocked me.

Another Thursday. For over a year the group in Billings had been praying for the woman with the severe problems of addiction. Once again they bowed their heads and said, "We know that in everything God works for good with [Sandy] who [loves] him" (Romans 8:28, RSV).

But at this meeting there was a difference: I was sitting among them.

On a bright June morning in 1979 I walked into a living room filled with smiling women who welcomed me warmly. My neighbor Kathy had invited me, and I perched nervously on the edge of a green sofa, waiting to see what all this "intercessory prayer" was about. I learned for the first time about the prayers that had gone up for me during my darkest days. I still needed much healing, but I was on my way.

Week after week I joined them in their prayers for others and for myself. Then, when I left Billings once again for a treatment center and halfway house, they continued their prayers. And later when I moved to Vermont to start a new life in 1983, I continued to call or write them. Their prayers were making a difference in my life, and I knew it.

Today I am living, breathing proof that prayers for others—intercessory prayers—are one of the most powerful tools that God has placed in our hands. My recovery did not take place in a month, or even a year. It was a long process.

Even nowadays, every so often, the tendency toward addictive behavior beckons me back to the old habits. It's then that I say my own prayer: "I, Sandy, can do all things through Christ who strengthens me." Then I bow my head, insert somebody else's name—and pass the prayer along for another.

Prayer Binds Us Together

JANET CHANDLER ESCOTT

When our two-year-old daughter Catherine was rushed to the hospital during a severe asthmatic attack, the doctor warned me that she was very close to death. I paced the hospital corridor, begging God to spare her.

Suddenly, I felt two arms around my shoulders and looked into the motherly face of a Mennonite woman. "I saw them wheel in your daughter," she said. "I've been praying for her. I know God will make her well again."

Her words touched me. "And you, why are *you* here?" I asked.

"My son was hit by a car, and though one of his legs had to be amputated, he survived and is recovering."

How strange. I'd read about that accident in the local newspaper—and had been so moved that I'd knelt and prayed intensely for the youngster. And now here was that boy's mother saying she'd prayed just as hard for *my* child.

Catherine pulled through. And my new friend, Mrs.

Shenk, and I both thanked God for showing us the truth of 1 Corinthians 12: We *are* all one body in Christ, and when one member suffers—or rejoices—the whole body does the same.

And prayer is the tie that binds that body together.

Prayer for the Helpless

Let me be a voice for the speechless,
Those who are small and weak;
Let me speak for all helpless creatures
Who have no power to speak.
I have lifted my heart to heaven
On behalf of the least of these—
The frightened, the homeless, the hungry.
I am voicing their pleas.
If I can help any creature,
Respond to a desperate call,
I will know that my prayer has been answered
By the God who created them all.

HELEN INWOOD

Prayer at the End of the Rope

O Lord,
never suffer us to think
that we can stand by ourselves,
and not need Thee.

John Donne (1572–1631)

The Prayer of Helplessness

CATHERINE MARSHALL

When I lived in the nation's Capital, I used to notice how often the Washington papers reported suicide leaps from the Calvert Street bridge. In fact, this happens so repeatedly that the site is often called "suicide bridge."

Sensing the human drama behind these brief notices—like the plunge of the young wife who had inoperable cancer, or that of the elderly man whose wife had just died—I often thought that if I could speak with such persons at the zero hour, I would try to stop them with the thought that helplessness is one of the greatest assets a human being can have.

For I believe that the old cliché "God helps those who help themselves" is not only misleading, but often dead wrong. My most spectacular answers to prayers have come when I could do nothing at all for myself.

The Psalmist says, "When I was hemmed in, thou hast freed me often" (Psalm 4:1, Moffatt). Gradually I have learned to recognize this hemming-in as one of God's most loving devices for teaching us that He is real and gloriously adequate for our problems.

One such experience occurred during the writing of my first book. As the young widow of Peter Marshall, Chaplain of the Senate, I was attempting what many felt was the rather audacious project of writing his biography. About midway in the manuscript, I received devastating criticism from one whose judgment I trusted. His words "You haven't even begun to get inside the man Peter Marshall" brought home to me the fact that unless God wrote this book through me, it would be a failure. The realization of my inadequacy as a writer was not only an intellectual one. It was also emotional; there were plenty of tears.

In my helplessness, there was no alternative but to put the project into God's hands. I prayed that *A Man Called Peter* be His book, and that the results be all His too.

And they were. I still regard as incredible the fact that I hear from time to time of lives changed through a book; of men entering the ministry through the inspiration of Peter Marshall's life.

More recently I saw the prayer of helplessness work in an everyday type situation—the matter of household help. Before my marriage to Leonard LeSourd in the fall of 1959, I was full of trepidation at the thought of taking on the care of three young children. My son Peter John had been away at school for over three years, and I had involved myself with a writing career. In his efforts to reassure me, Len was blithe with promises of household help.

But the help situation in Chappaqua proved unbelievably tight. Months passed. One woman stayed a few weeks, then left. We tried the Help Columns without success; persistent prayer brought us no nearer a solution. I finally decided I would have to do it all myself, but soon found it was more than a full-time job just running a lively household, not to mention my writing commitments.

So—once again the old familiar pattern ... the prayer of helplessness ... the admission that I could not do everything myself ... then the insight that my main responsibility was to our home. If God wanted me to resume my writing, He would show me the way.

After that admission of helplessness, Lucy Arsenault was sent to us—Lucy—steady, reliable, loyal, a jewel of a cook, a jewel of a person.

Why would God insist on helplessness as a prerequisite to answered prayer? One reason may be because our human helplessness is bedrock fact. Where God is left out of one's life, self-sufficiency is a complete delusion.

What is the truth? Not one of us had anything to do with his being born; no control over whether he is male or female, Japanese or Russian or American, white or yellow or black. Nor can we influence our ancestry, nor our basic mental or physical equipment.

After we are born, an autonomic nervous system controls every vital function that sustains life. A power that no one really understands keeps our heart beating, our lungs breathing, our blood circulating, our body temperature up.

A surgeon can cut tissues, but he is helpless to force

the body to bind the severed tissue together again.

We grow old relentlessly and automatically.

Self-sufficient? Hardly!

And the planet on which we live ... we are helpless there too. The little planet Earth is exactly the right distance—some 92 million miles—from the source of its heat and light. Any nearer, and we would be consumed with solar radiation; any further and we would be frozen to death. The balance of oxygen and nitrogen in the air we breathe is exactly right. The law of gravity operates. And man—little man who struts and fumes upon the earth—self-sufficient? Not at all ...

Did Jesus have any comment to make about all this? Yes, He put His finger on the heart of the matter as always: "Without me ye can do nothing," He said (John 15:5).

The setting for this sweeping statement by Jesus is the 15th chapter of John: "I am the true vine ... ye are the branches" (vss. 1, 5).

Dr. Arthur Gossip, who wrote the exposition on John for the famous Interpreter's Bible (Nashville: Abingdon Press) has this interesting comment: "These are surely the most hopeful words in Scripture ... *Apart from me, ye can do nothing.* For it is on the basis of that frank recognition of our utter fecklessness, apart from Him, that Christ ... gives us His great promises."

Helplessness? Utter fecklessness? Most of us do not enjoy admitting it. The cult of humanism in our day has trained us to believe that we are quite adequate to control our environment and to be masters of our own destiny.

Yet sometime in life, everyone of us finds ourself caught in circumstances that we are helpless to change. So in our physical world, and in our spiritual life, the scriptural statement is true: "A man can receive nothing, except it be given him from heaven" (John 3:27). He must have meant that an omnipotent, transcendent, and imminent God is above all and through all far more completely than we realize.

I have always been impressed by the story of Dr. A. B. Simpson, a famous New York preacher. Poor health had haunted this man. Two nervous breakdowns plus a heart condition led a famous New York physician to tell him that his days were numbered. Simpson was then only thirty-eight.

The physician's diagnosis only underscored the physical helplessness that the minister knew only too well. ... Always he preached with great effort. Climbing stairs or even a slight elevation was a suffocating agony of breathlessness.

It was at Old Orchard, Maine, that Dr. Simpson attended a unique religious service which sent him back to his Bible to find out for himself about Christ's attitude towards disease. He became convinced that Jesus had always meant healing to be a part of His gospel for the redemption of total being.

Soon after this revelation, Dr. Simpson took a walk. Coming to a pine woods, he sat down on a log to rest. Soon he found himself praying, telling God of his complete helplessness with regard to his physical condition. He then asked Christ to enter him and to become his physical life for all the needs of his body, until his lifework was done.

"There in the woods, I made a connection with God," he said later. "Every fiber in me was tingling with the sense of God's presence."

A few days after that, Simpson climbed a mountain three thousand feet high. "When I reached the top," he related joyfully, "the world of weakness and fear was lying at my feet. From that time I had literally a new heart in my breast."

And so he did. For the rest of his life, he was noted for the amazing volume of his pastoral and literary work. He lived to be seventy-six.

Now why does the prayer of helplessness work this way? Because trouble can be the starting point for both spiritual power and creativity. Creativity may be defined as the ability to combine old means into some new form. It is only when old ways of doing things are forcibly broken up by need or suffering that we are compelled to rethink, to begin again. Then the creative process begins to flow.

Fritz Kunkel, the eminent psychologist, puts it like this in his book *How Character Develops,* written with Roy Dickerson (New York: Scribners, 1940, pp. 131–32):

"The way to real creativeness is through danger or suffering. ... He who ... relies upon his own small private consciousness must fail, for the source of creativity is not the individual but the We, or to state it another way, the God who manifests Himself in the We. ..."

To one beset by difficulty and discouragement, here

are three suggestions for finding help through the prayer of helplessness.

First, be honest with God. Tell Him that you are aware of the fact that in His eyes you are helpless. Give God permission to make you feel your helplessness *at the emotional level,* if that's what He wants. And recognize that this may be painful. There is good psychological reason why this first step is necessary. Unless the power of our emotions is touched, it is as if a fuse remains unlit.

Second, take your heart's desire to God. You have accepted your helplessness. Now grip with equal strength of will your belief that God can do through you what you cannot. It may seem to you for a time that you are relying on emptiness, dangling over a chasm. Disregard these feelings, and quietly thank God that He is working things out.

Third, watch now for opening doors and opportunities for creativity. When the right door opens, you will have a quiet inner assurance that God's hand is on the knob. That is the time of action for you, for the beginning of the most creative period you have ever known.

An Enchanted Place

LINDA ANDERSON

That September morning, I sat in our trailer deep in the mountains of north Georgia, reading to my daughter BJ, who'd stayed home from school with a headache. It was just the two of us. My husband, Boyd, a teacher, had left for work, and our younger children, Annmarie and John, had caught the school bus. I'd planned to work on the log house Boyd and I were building near the trailer, but I was happy to spend the morning with BJ instead.

Born with a rare condition called Rubenstein-Taybi Syndrome, BJ was mentally retarded. At seventeen she had a big smile and an exuberance for life that spilled over to everyone around her. Her physical mobility wasn't restricted. She attended a school for the handicapped. At home she loved to jump happy somersaults on the trampoline beside the trailer. Sometimes I even forgot what the doctors down in Atlanta had told us—that BJ probably wouldn't live past sixteen. It certainly never occurred to me that morning that BJ's headache was anything to worry about.

She leaned back on my shoulder as I turned the pages of her favorite book, *The Secret Garden.* We read about an enchanted place hidden behind an ivy-covered wall and how it transformed the life of a lonely, miserable girl who found it. As the story ended, BJ closed her eyes.

While she napped I gazed through the window at our log house. It had always been my dream to build a home beneath the misting, blue-green mountains I'd known since I was a child. The mountains were part of me, sure as my hands and feet. They cradled memories of Daddy playing "Red Wing" on his fiddle, midwife Fanny Wilson hurrying to deliver a baby, and folks praying on their knees in the little mountain church. But mostly the mountains reminded me of the old tenant house where I'd lived as a child. I remembered clear as yesterday the room with the glowing potbellied stove, the smell of sage drying on the wall, and the stick on Mama's butter churn making music.

But there were hard memories too. Mama had gone to work as a maid to feed us children after Daddy died. She'd even taken in ironing at night and gone hungry so we could eat. I marveled at how she'd handled so much hardship, and I'd been inclined to chalk it up to her own indomitable spirit. But Mama had believed it was God who saw her through. "When difficulties come, you only have to call out to God and He'll be right there helping you," she always told me.

As the old memories drifted away, I turned from the

window and found BJ waking up. She stood and walked down the hall of the trailer toward the bathroom. I watched with a small, perplexed frown. She was walking strangely, swaying, wobbling. Yet before I could move, before I could draw another breath, BJ fell to the floor.

Her body jerked with a violent convulsion. I was a licensed practical nurse, but there was nothing I could do to stop it. When the seizure finally subsided, BJ was unconscious, and nothing in our lives would ever be the same again.

The doctor told Boyd and me she'd had a terrible stroke and the damage to her brain was permanent. She would live, but she wouldn't talk or walk or do anything ever again. Because of my nurse's training, the doctor suggested I care for her at home, and that was the only way Boyd and I wanted it. Besides, there was no way we could afford anything else, even with Boyd teaching a full schedule of electronics classes at North Georgia Technical School. The medical bills were already staggering, especially with the debt on our log house.

It wasn't quite complete, but we moved into the house so BJ could have a big room of her own. And it was there I began my endless vigils by her bed. She had to have care every minute, to be fed, changed and bathed. It took hours to spoon liquid food into her mouth because of her tendency to choke. But worst of all were the seizures.

BJ suffered one or two convulsions a day, and sometimes so many I stopped counting. Each time one came I gave her the injection prescribed by the doctor and fought to keep her breathing. When it was over, she lay so still and blue that I would touch her heart to see if she was still alive.

Caring for BJ became the only world I knew. I wasn't able to leave the house even to go to the barn. I saw the mountains only from the windows, and gradually I stopped seeing them at all. BJ became more and more of a burden. Inside I ached for the laughing girl who bounced on the trampoline and burrowed her head against my shoulder while we read *The Secret Garden.* But that girl was gone forever.

Meanwhile the bills mounted. I put hand-me-downs on the children, and Boyd raised vegetables in the garden and took a second job. Thank goodness most of our creditors were like the man at the hardware store, who said he'd wait till we could pay him back. It seemed to me he would be waiting forever.

As the months dragged by I dwindled to ninety-eight pounds, with raccoon circles under my eyes; my spirit withered. Finally one winter night more than two years after BJ's stroke, I reached the absolute end of my strength. It was 2:00 A.M. and BJ was caught in the grip of a convulsion that seemed to go on forever. When it ended I placed the oxygen mask over her face to draw the color of life back into her, then sank into a chair, lower than I'd ever been in my life. I'd tried to manage by myself, but I knew I could not go on. *What am I gonna do?* I thought. I cried like a child. And suddenly I found myself thinking about Mama, about her simple belief that God would come and help in difficulty if only we called on Him.

Utterly helpless, I fell on my knees and began to pray, feeling the words come from a place so deep inside of me that it seemed to have no bottom. "Dearest God, I need You," I cried. "I accept the difficulty life has handed me. But please, help me. Just send me some way to cope with it."

The moon's light was streaming through the window. I watched it, a downy sort of light, and a soft feeling of peace stole over me. In my mind I saw God bending over me and BJ as if we were two chicks.

The next morning I rubbed the sleep out of my eyes and peered out BJ's window. Everything seemed dipped in a kind of radiance. Pine trees appeared to my eyes like cones of the greenest green I'd ever seen. I looked down at the brown heart of a sunflower near the porch, noticing the way it spiraled like a staircase. I was seeing shapes and intricacies I'd never noticed before. Colors seemed brighter, images more vivid. I knew God had come in the night and unveiled my eyes! I shook my head, bewildered by what it meant.

"Something good's gonna happen," I told Boyd at the breakfast table. The flicker of faith I'd felt the night before had ignited into an overpowering anticipation that God was somehow going to answer my prayer for a way to cope. Boyd smiled. It was the first hope he'd seen in me in months.

A week later my sister, Barbara, came to visit. She found me by BJ's bed looking through the window. "Why don't you paint a picture?" she said out of the blue.

"Paint a picture?" I'd never painted anything but the faces on some dolls I'd made once.

"Why not?" Barbara said. "I'll bring you some canvases. Just promise me you'll paint something you know about."

I thought about the mysterious gift of seeing that had come to me in the night, and somehow I knew my sister's voice was really God's. *Paint a picture,* He was saying.

"I could paint what I love," I said, thinking about my life in the mountains, about the little mountain church, about Daddy and his fiddle, and Mama beating out a rhythm on her butter churn.

Suddenly pictures were flashing in my head bolder and faster than I could take them in. I was seeing them the way I'd seen the pine trees and the sunflower from BJ's window. I was seeing them with some kind of holy fire in my eyes.

The next day as I sat with BJ, I propped a seventy-nine-cent canvas atop my lap and began to paint. I painted the room of my childhood: the black wood stove glowing with a red light, sage drying on the wall, the old butcher-block table laden with molded butter. In the center I painted Mama at her butter churn, and in the corner, a window with snow falling hard outside.

From time to time I looked up from the canvas to BJ, mystified by what was happening. For the more I painted, the more I seemed to be inside that room, drawing up warmth and quietness and love. And it came to me: that room was really a place inside my own heart, a transforming place like the secret garden in BJ's storybook. I knew that through this gift of painting, God was giving me a refuge where I could find the peace and strength to cope with the harshness on the outside.

Through the spring and summer I painted mountain images by BJ's bed, and every day I felt myself gaining new strength. I began to find peace in caring for BJ, thanking God for the things He allowed me to do for her.

By summer's end something wondrous was happening to BJ too. Gradually she began taking most of her meals without choking. And one day the seizures simply stopped. Her cheeks grew pink as rose petals. She was still inside her own silent world, but I could tell by her face that BJ was finally at peace.

Her improvement allowed me to get out some. As Labor Day approached, a friend called and invited me to participate in an arts-and-crafts show in Homer, the Banks County seat. "You could sell some of those dolls you made," she suggested.

I agreed, hoping I could sell enough to buy school shoes for the children. But after I hung up, an unexpected idea sparked in my head: *Take your paintings.* The thought came again and again.

So on the day of the show, Boyd carted more than twenty of my pictures over in his old truck. I set them out, wondering if the $35 I was asking was too much. Then I bent over my easel to finish one more painting to add to the others.

"Hello, I'm Dr. Burrison from Atlanta," a voice behind me said. "And I don't think you're asking a fair price."

My throat went dry from embarrassment as I turned to find a distinguished-looking man studying my pictures. "Well, I didn't rightly know what to ask," I said apologetically.

"Oh, no," he said. "You should be asking a lot more."

He was, it seemed, a specialist in folk art, and he wanted to give my name to an art dealer in Atlanta. I think that astonished me even more than what happened right afterward: a woman came by and bought every single painting I had—even the half-finished one on the easel.

True to his word, Dr. Burrison contacted the art dealer, and less than a year later I was having a real art show at the Alexander Gallery in Atlanta. Amazingly, it was a sellout, and since then other shows have followed. And the thing I thought would never happen did—we paid back the man at the hardware store and began to put our financial burdens behind us.

Today I have a whole new life. I paint near BJ's bed, caring for her as always. But she is no longer a burden; she is a joy. Most important, I have learned a simple truth, one Mama knew all along: that there is no difficulty so big or so dark that God cannot help us find a way to deal with it. His strong peace is hidden away in the most unlikely places in our lives. And if we ask, He will come and set it free to sing inside us like the music of a butter churn.

The Marvelous Calf-Rope Principle

DOROTHY SHELLENBERGER

My husband Charles and I were driving my Uncle Frank, age eighty-five, arthritic old saint, lovable as a puppy, stubborn as a mule, and deaf as a post, back to his Oklahoma farm. The three of us had shared a near-perfect two-week holiday in Colorado.

It was Father's Day. Our plan was to drop Uncle Frank at his old homestead outside Oklahoma City and then make it back to our home in Waco, Texas, where our four grown children and their families would join us for dinner.

We had stopped to call Clara, the woman who cooked meals and took care of Uncle Frank, to ask if she would mind preparing a light lunch for the three of us. But a woman I didn't know had answered. After much hemming and hawing, she informed me that Clara had suddenly married an old sweetheart and departed. "Ma'am," the woman said, "I don't know nothin' else. Clara asked me to come in this morning and feed the animals. She left you all a note."

Uncle Frank and Charles were waiting in the car when I came outside. I crawled in the back seat feeling like someone had socked me in the stomach. Charles turned questioning eyes in my direction, but I silenced him with a shake of my head and an uplifted palm.

"Will Clara fix some of my gen-u-wine garden tomatoes for lunch?" Uncle Frank asked, completely unaware that anything was wrong.

"I forgot to ask," I mumbled.

How was I going to break the news? How would my old uncle, so crippled with arthritis he could hardly walk, manage without Clara on whom he had depended for years? As the miles melted behind us, I weighed alternatives.

I couldn't put him in a nursing home, even temporarily. In his delirium following major hip surgery three years ago he kept repeating, "Girl, you won't put me in a rest home, will you?"

When finally he was fully conscious, I had promised, "Uncle Frank, unless the day should come when you wouldn't know the difference anyway, I give you my solemn word that I will never put you in a rest home."

Moving him to Waco to live with us wasn't a satisfactory alternative either. For years Uncle Frank had lived with his sister, my mother. When Mother died, we had offered to recreate his den and bedroom in our empty boys' room.

"Can I bring Blanche and Julie and Kate and Martha and Bess and Annie?" he asked mischievously, naming his registered Holstein cows. "And can I bring Dot?" Dot was his Border Collie dog named after me. "How about my chickens on your city lot? No, girl, if the day ever comes that I have to move away from all my old friends, both two-legged and four-legged, I hope it is my last ... I pray to God every night He'll let me stay right here till the day I die."

Uprooting Uncle Frank was not the answer.

Miles back, Charles had turned on the car radio, but now Uncle Frank interrupted its drone. "Boy" (we had grandchildren, but Charles was still "boy" to him), "turn off that blasted radio. Dorothy hasn't spoken one word since she called Clara. Something's wrong. Has anythin' happened to Dot?" Dot was getting old, too.

Then, I had to tell him the whole story—that Clara was gone.

His voice was almost a whisper. "No wonder she wanted me to come on this trip so much." ... Twenty miles later, "She ironed up all my shirts ... said I had enough to last a year." ... Another fifteen miles ... "Did you notice she gave me a little peck on the cheek when we left? She's never done that before. She was plannin' on leavin'."

By the time we reached El Reno, Uncle Frank had dozed off, and Charles and I talked. He said I should stay with Uncle Frank and try to find a housekeeper. He would go on home to be with the children and grandchildren on Father's Day. "It's not going to be easy finding someone who will be conscientious about staying with an eighty-five-year-old man," he said.

"I've got a few aces up my sleeve," I said. "Maybe it won't be too difficult."

"I'll be praying for you, dear."

"Okay, honey, you do the praying and I'll do the work," I answered glibly.

An hour later, Uncle Frank was having a loving reunion with his Border Collie dog and his big cat "Tom." He ate the lunch I prepared and limped out to look over his beloved land.

I kissed Charles good-bye and reassured him I'd be home in a few days.

Monday morning I called the church where Uncle Frank had worshiped for fifty years. The associate pastor came over with the entire church roll; together we looked for a widowed lady who might like to have a relatively easy job with good pay and a snug little home in the guest house. We didn't come up with one interested person.

Tuesday morning I went to nearby Yukon, a Czech community where Uncle Frank had done business for as long as I could remember. Today it is a major extension of Oklahoma City, and the "good Czech people" who had once saved their money were now enjoying spending it. All the thrifty widows I had envisioned hiring were off on summer tours of Europe.

Wednesday I stayed on the phone all day, calling friends and acquaintances, anyone I thought might give me a lead. "A dependable housekeeper?" one good friend laughed. "Dorothy, you have to be kidding. They disappeared before the miniskirt."

On Thursday I placed a "Help Wanted" ad in the *Daily Oklahoman.*

The ad ran for two weeks and netted two applicants.

One never showed up for her appointment. The other was so slovenly I was afraid to let her in.

What was worse, I was beginning to resent Uncle Frank. He was as calm as if my being there were permanent. Every night after puttering around the place all day, he listened to the ten o'clock news, read his Bible for a while and trundled off to bed, falling asleep as soon as his head hit the pillow. I was tossing and turning for hours before dropping off in a restless sleep.

The morning of July 3, we were sitting at the breakfast table. Uncle Frank usually said a simple grace. But this morning he called on me, and suddenly I was pouring out my heart. "Lord," I prayed, "I'm at the end of my rope. I don't know what to do. I can't stay here, and I can't go home. I love Uncle Frank, Lord, but I know You love him more than I do. Would You please take charge here? Thank You. Amen."

When I raised my head, Uncle Frank was smiling. "Well, girl, now that you've learned the calf-rope principle, we can expect a miracle."

"The calf-rope principle?" I asked numbly. "What's that?"

"Dorothy, you know whenever you need to brand a calf or treat it for some disease, you've got to lasso that little critter first. You know he'll run as if you were a coyote wantin' him for supper. It's only when he's reached the end of his rope that you can do what's best for him. Well, girl, it's the same way with the Lord. Long as we want to do things our way, He lets us. When we come to the end of our rope and are willin' for Him to take over, that's when we can depend on Him to do what's best for us. And we can thank Him, too, knowin' He's gonna work it out to His glory and for our good."

"Who taught you the calf-rope principle, Uncle Frank?"

"David did—in the Psalms. He wrote, 'When I was pinned down, You have freed me often.' " (Uncle Frank's interpretation of Psalm 4:1.)

"When did you apply the calf-rope principle to our predicament?" I asked.

"Comin' home, somewhere between Elk City and El Reno."

"Then why is it taking so long to get an answer?"

"The Lord was waitin' on you to learn the principle, too," he said.

Mulling over Uncle Frank's words after breakfast, a name popped into my head. Tom Little.

Tom was the son-in-law of friends of ours in Waco. He and his wife, Becky, and their two boys were living in Oklahoma City when my mother died, but they had moved to Greenville, Texas, shortly afterward. Hadn't Tom recently been transferred back to Oklahoma City? Hadn't I heard that Tom was living in one room because he and Becky hadn't been able to sell their home in Greenville? Hadn't Tom been the one who had said that his dream was to live on a farm like this someday?

A telephone call verified all my questions, and the next day, July 4, Tom and Rebecca Little and their two teenage boys, Tommy and Bruce, drove up from Texas to see us.

Nothing was said to Uncle Frank about their coming. They just dropped by for a friendly visit "since they were in town for the Fourth." But when they left I just knew that they were coming back.

"Uncle Frank," I said, picking up the empty lemonade glasses in his den, "what would you think about sharing this big house with the Littles? Tom was raised on a farm. Becky is a good cook. You would have your den and bath and bedroom and join them for meals. The boys seem so courteous and cheerful. What do you think?"

Uncle Frank turned his blue eyes to meet mine. "Dorothy," he paused a long time, "sometimes this past year, I've been so lonesome in this big empty house, I've turned the radio up just to keep me company. Clara has been bringin' my meals in since your mother died. I've eaten alone for the past year ... Did you hear Bruce askin' me about the Oklahoma Run? ... Tommy plays the guitar—that's my favorite. I'm sure willin' to give it a try if they are. When can they move in?"

Through tears I said, "Next week."

I'd never realized how lonesome Uncle Frank had been since my mother's death.

The Little family gave Uncle Frank two of the happiest years of his life. He died in October 1972, but they are still there eight years later, taking care of the old home place that he loved so much, the house where Uncle Frank lived out every day of his full life and taught others how to live by the principles of the Word.

A Letter from Death Row

ANNE PURDY

Our home is in a truly isolated gold region of northern Alaska, up a two-hundred-mile stretch of mountainous road. There is no school, no church.

For ten years I taught school classes gratis in my house to Indian, Eskimo and Caucasian children. Living conditions were intolerable for some of them. Having a big house and no children, we adopted ten and raised them as our own.

But there were others who needed help and there wasn't much we could do for some of these.

One boy, William Albert Tahl, used to come to our house whenever he was upset with troubles at home. Art, as he was called, would stay with us for a few days until things quieted down and then he'd go home. Art first came to us when he was eleven but he returned often through the years. We tried to help with school lessons, clothes, food, outings and provide him with love.

But Art had deep wounds inside that love could not heal. Late in his teens Art left home for good, and for years I did not hear from him. Then I received the following letter:

Dear Teacher:

Perhaps you don't even remember me from your classroom and home over fifteen years ago. I remember you so very well. It's a long, ugly story, but I won't bother you with details.

I am in Death Row awaiting execution. In a drunken rage I committed murder. I deserve to die and it's okay, but one thing bothers me. I'm afraid of what comes after death. I know you believe in God and prayer and that is why I ask your help now.

In other words, I cannot face what lies beyond with guilt on my soul and no hope of forgiveness. If you still believe in God, write and give me the courage to face death.

Your friend, Art Tahl

After reading this letter I sat stunned for a while. How well I remembered the handsome lad with his charming manners and light-hearted disposition despite his troubles.

Taking a day and night to think it over and choosing my words carefully, I wrote Art, assuring him of my friendship and interest. In closing I said, "We are forgiven until seventy times seven and Christ died on the cross for the remission of our sins. Remember He said 'Though your sins be as scarlet, they shall be as white as snow' (Isaiah

1:18). With God all things are possible; you need only to turn to Him."

From the agony of his tortured soul, the condemned man began writing his innermost thoughts and fears. It was almost as though I looked into his heart and understood the sorrow and tribulation written there.

I answered the letters regularly, sending religious cards and poems. I also sent scriptural passages. Art followed my advice and read the Bible daily. Day and night I prayed for him.

As time dragged on for Art, I sensed a gradual change in his spirit. His letters were more hopeful. In one letter he made a remark I'll remember for a long time:

"I've always thought about myself first in everything. There are 58 men due to go to the gas chamber the same as I. Lately I think of and pray for them and I can even smile at the guards and pray for them too. My last act at night and my first when I awake is to pray that God will bless and help all the unfortunate people in the world."

Now was the appointed time for a very special letter. I sat down and wrote to Art without thinking it out; words poured from my pen:

Dear Art:

You are now ready for the great step. Take a large sheet of paper and write down all the crimes of your life, your fears and hopes. Lay all your sins on God's altar. When the lights are out and the guards are gone, get down on your knees and say, "God, here it is, all of it. You need no light for You are the light of the world. Forgive me, Father."

Destroy the paper. Never divulge the contents to anyone. Complete forgiveness, and abiding faith, a cleanliness of mind, body and soul will be given you to last through Eternity.

Anne Purdy

I soon received an answer to my letter.

Dear Teacher:

I followed your instructions perfectly. I want you to know because you love me regardless of everything. I stayed on my knees all night praying. I wasn't conscious of time or anything, only of God's forgiveness and love pouring over my guilty soul.

When the guard came with breakfast I lay on the floor as though dead. The man stared at me, turned white, fear showed in his eyes. "You okay?" he choked out.

I nodded and smiled. The guard looked at me again. "My God," he gasped, "there's a light on your face." He set the tray down and fled.

Through God's grace I am clean, clean. I could shout it from the housetops. Thanks for bringing me to God. I'm not afraid anymore, of death or the hereafter.

Editor's note: Art Tahl was not executed in 1967, when this story was published, but was finally released in 1987.

I am condemned to die in the gas chamber. I am ready, God is with me. My body will die but not my soul. All is well, strong and sure. I go forth to meet my God.

Art Tahl

Hands

Hands express many things ...
Sorrow, gladness, fear.
Hands can push someone away,
Or hold them very near.

Hands create beautiful things
And some hands can destroy.
Hands can spank a naughty child
Or mend his broken toy.

But there's another use for hands,
Which everyone can afford.
And that's when you reach out and say,
"Take my hand, please, Lord."

JAMES D. SMITH
U. S. PENITENTIARY, LEAVENWORTH, KANSAS

UNEXPECTED ANSWERS

The Good No

So often our self-centered prayers,
If granted, could bring only woe.
How glad we should be that God cares,
And loves us enough to say, "No."

MARY HAMLETT GOODMAN

When Your Prayers Seem Unanswered

CONSTANCE FOSTER

What are we to conclude when we have prayed for a long time and nothing seems to be any different from before? Is God whimsical, given to listening to one person but turning a deaf ear on another, or hearing us on some occasions and ignoring us on others? Many people ask themselves these questions. When they pray and things remain much the same or even grow worse, they may come to the conclusion that prayer is at best uncertain and at worst futile.

I became so much interested in this subject of apparently unanswered prayer that for several years now I have been gathering records of such instances.

Carol W. was a young college student when she first came to my attention. In spite of hard work and great ambition, Carol was failing to make passing grades in certain subjects and had been warned that unless she did well on her term examinations, she would be dropped at the end of the year. Carol was praying sincerely for success in her exams. But a month later she phoned me and her first words were, "Well, I prayed but nothing happened."

Carol had flunked two courses and the college dropped her. Certainly surface appearances here would seem to justify her conclusion that "nothing happened" as the result of prayer. But wait! And never forget that God knows more than we do about what is for our highest good.

A few weeks after she returned home, Carol consulted a psychologist who was an expert at determining in what areas an individual's best talents lay. He gave her a battery of aptitude tests that revealed she was extremely gifted in spatial perception and mechanical ability. They also showed that she was not naturally a good student where abstract subjects, such as she had taken at college, were concerned.

Carol took a course at a technical school in X-ray therapy and medical techniques. Today she is head of a large hospital laboratory with a dozen assistants under her direction, making a splendid salary and happy in her work. Did nothing happen when she prayed? Graduation from a liberal arts college was not the right answer to her needs and abilities. Carol didn't know it. But God did.

Now let us turn to another example of apparently unanswered prayer. It concerns an elderly widow whose husband's death had left her almost destitute and in danger of losing her large home. She could no longer meet the heavy expense of maintaining it. Mrs. Horton wrote me for prayers that she might be able by some miracle to keep it, together with all her cherished possessions. A few months later another letter from her reached me. "We both prayed," she wrote, "but nothing happened." The house was to be sold at auction the following week. Mrs. Horton was heartbroken.

During the next few days Mrs. Horton went through her house with tear-stained eyes, sorting and discarding the accumulation of long years of living in it. In the attic she ran across an old stamp collection that had been in her husband's family for years. She almost threw it in the pile of rubbish. Of what use were a lot of old stamps? But something made her put it aside to save.

A year went by before she thought of it again. The house had been sold. "Nothing had happened." She was bitter. Her prayer had not been answered. Then one day she happened to see an advertisement in a large city newspaper, listing the value of certain rare stamps. Mrs. Horton made a special trip to see the dealer, carrying the old collection with her. When she left his office she was dazed and unbelieving, for in her purse she had his check for nearly $11,000!

The big old house had been much too large for one woman to care for comfortably. She did not need all that space. Today she realizes it. What she required was smaller living quarters together with enough money in the bank for her expenses. That is exactly what God gave her in answer to her supposedly "unanswered" prayer.

Then there was the businessman who had been praying for an increase in salary. Instead his company reshuffled its personnel and he was placed in a different department with a pay *decrease.* They told him he could leave if he was not satisfied to stay on at the lower figure.

He phoned me about the new development and his voice was bitter. "What good is prayer?" he demanded. This is just another variation on the "But nothing happened" theme. Where was God in all this, he wanted to know. Where indeed? Right where He always is, of course, busy making all things work together for good in our individual lives. Had nothing happened?

It seems that my friend had never before been engaged in selling but the new job gave him a chance to try his hand at it and he proved to have a genius for it. Today, three years later, he is sales manager for his firm at a salary five times larger than the one he was receiving when he first prayed for an increase. More important still, he is doing work that is productive and rewarding. Had he not been "demoted," the promotion could never have happened.

My final story concerns a very dear neighbor whose retarded child could not seem to learn. Betty came to me in great distress one day. "It's the last straw," she burst. "As if I didn't already have enough grief and trouble with poor little Karen, now I have to take in my husband's father. He's practically senile. Oh please pray as you never prayed before that we can get some other relative to take care of him."

But there was no other relative able to take in the old man. The day Grandpa arrived my neighbor echoed the same old sad refrain, "We prayed, but nothing happened. I'm stuck." Nothing happened? It looked that way, didn't it?

But God had something wonderful in store for that mother. He had the highest welfare of her retarded child at heart. For tiny Karen began to blossom in Grandpa's company. They seemed to understand each other and soon they were inseparable. Grandpa was not critical of her failings and never pushed her beyond her capacity. He accepted and loved her as she was and for herself alone.

For hours on end Karen sat in Grandpa's lap while he rocked and sang to her. She began to talk and laugh and play. Today she is a practically normal child and although the old man now is no longer living, the family is eternally grateful that God brought him to stay with them and love Karen into overcoming her handicap.

Make no mistake, there is no such thing as an unanswered prayer. God hears every whisper of our hearts but He loves us too much always to answer in the precise terms that we ask. He often has a better answer.

So never say "but nothing happened" when your prayers are not immediately fulfilled as you think they should be. Something always happens. A spiritual force has been set in motion that never stops vibrating in the universal atmosphere. A great chain reaction takes place which may not bring you exactly what you asked for, perhaps, but something infinitely better for your eternal advantage. In short, it is impossible for you to pray and then be able to say truthfully, "But nothing happened."

The Box

MARY LOUISE KITSEN

"There's more to do than I can handle," I said loudly and clearly. Of course, there was no one to hear my complaint except the three cats lying on the bed. Two of them continued sleeping while the third laid her ears back and switched her tail.

I sighed. There were writing assignments to be done (I'm a full-time freelance writer); my cousins were coming from Kansas in a few days and I felt I had to clean the entire house; and my mother was in the hospital again, which meant two trips there each day. How would I get to everything?

Deciding that Jesus was the only One who was listening, I addressed Him directly this time. "With Your help, I'll make it, but please, don't let anything else happen right now."

It was still early in the morning. I slipped my robe on and started downstairs. Maybe if I relaxed briefly with some toast and coffee, taking a look at the morning paper at the same time, I'd feel ready to tackle the busy day ahead. I opened the door and picked up the newspaper. Then I saw the box.

Where did it come from? It was a large box with "Corn-Flakes" written on the side. An old, rusted window screen lay on top; a rope kept it in place. Oh, no ... someone who knows how I feel about cats must have dumped some kittens on me again. Just what I needed!

I started to pick the box up, and when I felt how heavy it was, I thought. "They've dumped the mother cat too." Actually, I didn't know the half of it!

I set the box down in the living room, untied the rope and looked in. There was a big yellow cat. But where were her kittens? I reached in and lifted the cat out. It started to purr immediately and pushed its head tightly against my shoulder. One big cat? A male at that.

I held the cat up to take a better look at him. And started to sob. This big, beautiful cat had no eyes—just white skin where his eyes should have been. I cradled him as my other cats started to gather. Pip-Squeak rubbed against the newcomer with evident pleasure. But what was I going to do with a blind kitty? How much care would he need?

I looked in the box to see if there was anything else and found the note: "This is Poppy. My dad hates having him around and said he'd shoot him if Mom and I didn't get rid of him ourselves. Please take care of him." It was in the handwriting of a youngster. Poor, sad child trying to keep a blind cat alive.

Poppy ate with the other cats—to my surprise and relief—and I showed him the litter box. I got absolutely nothing done before it was time to leave for the hospital; and I worried about leaving the cat in a strange place. But he seemed content and interested in investigating things. I called the vet's office and made an appointment. Then I left, praying that Poppy would make out all right.

When I returned home, I found Poppy sleeping with Pip-Squeak in the sunny dining room window. In the early afternoon I put him in a carrier and headed for the vet's office. I hated to take him, but I had to have help in this matter. The vet took him into a back room to check him over. I sat straight as a pin, not knowing what to expect.

The vet finally came out. He was alone. My heart did a flip-flop. What about Poppy? At that moment I realized the big yellow cat had stolen my heart.

"Someone took good care of that fellow," the doctor told me. "He's in good shape and amazingly contented. We'll keep him a couple days. He should be altered and have some shots, and there are a few tests we'd like to do."

I grinned.

Then the bomb fell. "We think Poppy is deaf and dumb as well as blind."

For the next two days I wondered how I'd manage a pet that couldn't see, hear or make a sound. I prayed about the cat. And, to my surprise, I was getting an awful lot of things accomplished even though my mind stayed on Poppy. It was as though Poppy was a challenge and so everything else was a challenge too.

I brought Poppy and my mother home from their respective hospitals just two days later. I went for Mom first and got her settled in her favorite chair in the living room. Then I went for Poppy.

Mom moved to the edge of her chair as I brought the carrier in. I opened it and Poppy climbed into my arms. How he loved people! I carried him over to Mom and she gathered him to her. In minutes, Poppy purred happily on her lap. It was the start of a warm, personal friendship between an elderly lady and a handicapped kitty cat—a relationship that has made both of their lives happier.

Poppy had helped me too. I was feeling sorry for myself when he came, but through him I gained a better attitude. It seemed almost as if Jesus had helped guide Poppy's owners to the act of bringing him to me. Little by little I began to think more and more about the mother and child who had left Poppy in my care. Who were they? Would they wonder about what had happened to Poppy?

And then one day I made a sign that said "Poppy is fine" and taped it to my front porch. I hoped the youngster who had brought the cat to me would see it.

The sign stayed up for several days. Then came the morning I went outside to the garage and I saw something that made my life even better. Written on the bottom of the sign I'd made were two messages, evidently written by the child and his mother—or that's what I've always thought. The child's writing said, "Thank you." The adult's hand wrote, "God Bless You."

I Asked for Bread

AUTHOR UNKNOWN

I asked for bread; God gave a stone instead.
Yet, while I pillowed there my weary head,
The angels made a ladder of my dreams,
Which upward to celestial mountains led.
And when I woke beneath the morning's beams,
Around my resting place fresh manna lay;
And, praising God, I went upon my way.
For I was fed.

God answers prayer; sometimes when hearts are weak,
He gives the very gifts believers seek.
But often faith must learn a deeper rest,
And trust God's silence when He does not speak;
For He whose name is Love will send the best.
Stars may burn out, nor mountain walls endure,
But God is true, His promises are sure
For those who seek.

First Year of Teaching

SARAH BRADFORD*

I looked at the blond teenager slumped at his desk in the back row of my classroom and felt sick inside.

Only six weeks ago, before I started my first year of teaching English to college freshmen, I had prayed, "God, please send me students who need what I can give." And now I asked despairingly, "Why, Lord? Why did You send me Robby?"

There was absolutely nothing I could give this student. I suspected strongly that he was an alcoholic, and that was a disease I'd had no luck coping with.

When I stopped at his desk to return a paper he'd handed in, it was clear that he'd been drinking before class. Once again he smelled like a brewery; his eyes were bloodshot; his hair, disheveled. My words tumbled out before I

*Names have been changed.

could stop them. "Robby, are you in the habit of drinking beer for breakfast?"

I regretted the sarcasm but couldn't control my frustration. I felt as angry and helpless as I had been on a Christmas Eve during my childhood when my father staggered into the tree on his way to the kitchen for another beer. Ornaments shattered on the hardwood floor, and the colored lights sputtered and went out. After my mother helped him up, he still got that beer. "Mama, don't you ever want to g-give up?" I asked in an unsteady voice. She sighed. "He needs me to stand by him and pray for him. With God's help, somehow, someway ... well, I know he'll find his way."

Now, in my classroom, Robby looked at his desk and shoved both hands into the pockets of his jeans. "I'm rushing a fraternity," he muttered. "You must smell beer from the party last night."

I shook my head. "Robby, you've already missed three classes." I held out the theme he'd written. "And a D on your first paper isn't a good way to start the semester."

He looked up pleadingly. "But I won't be absent anymore. I promise. And I'll work harder on my next paper."

Classes were changing, and before I could respond, he had risen and disappeared into the crowd. I walked briskly down the hall to my office. I hated myself for being angry and blamed Robby for making me feel that way.

He's just like my father, I thought. He was unreachable. Irresponsible. How many times had I tried to get through to my father—to no avail? And then more heartbreak—my younger brother started drinking. Again and again I'd begged him to stop, bailed him out of jail, listened to his lame excuses. All for nothing. My heels drummed on the terrazzo floor of the hall. Robby would have to solve his own problems, I decided. I had nothing left to give.

For the next several weeks, Robby did come to class regularly. Slumping at a desk in the back left-hand corner of my classroom, he daydreamed or gazed out the window into bright leaves and sunshine. Sometimes he'd get up during a class discussion to go outside and drink from the water fountain.

The two papers he handed in looked as if they'd been dashed off. I marked a large D on each. Yet when I lectured or led discussions, I'd find myself looking back to Robby's corner of the classroom. His eyes carefully avoided my gaze; sometimes he'd flinch, as if recoiling from a punch.

When I handed back Robby's fourth assignment, I watched him open it to the back page. His eyes fell on the inevitable D, and I saw tears well in his eyes.

They always cry, I thought bitterly, remembering how my father's large hands would shake as he'd cover his face and say he was sorry and promise to change. Now, for some reason, I felt guilty, as if I were the cause of Robby's misery. I quickly caught myself. I would not be manipulated into feeling responsible. *"He's* got to take responsibility," I vowed.

Determined to confront him, I caught him at the door after class. "Robby, can we talk a minute?" I asked. He looked at the floor and didn't answer. "I—I don't like giving

D's," I began, "but you haven't given me much choice."

"I can't write like you want," he muttered. "Whatever it is you want, I can't do it."

I stiffened. *That's always it,* I thought. Blame anything but the alcohol. Just give up. Expect to be bailed out. "Robby, you could write perfectly well," I found myself saying, "if you'd stop drinking and start caring about your work."

He looked up at me. "I hate the paper topics," he countered. "They're stupid."

Paper topics were under the control of the English Department and I assigned what the syllabus demanded. Now Robby wanted me to make an exception for him. I hated exceptions. I stared at Robby; for a fleeting moment I recalled my mother's eyes, warm and steady, reflecting her conviction. I could hear her saying firmly, "We won't give up on your father. We'll go on believing that God can give him the will to change." Something broke within me—or maybe I was just tired of being angry, unsure of what to do next. I knew what Mama would do.

Robby poked nervously at a hole in his faded jeans, shuffled his feet and waited for me to respond. Then, obviously anxious to retreat, he tried to edge past me. "It's not your problem," he said. "You can just flunk me and forget it."

But I stood there blocking his path. He was wrong. It *was* my problem. I remembered the prayer I'd said before school began. I hadn't asked God for the best students but for those who needed what I could give.

I took a deep breath. "Okay, Robby, on the next paper

you can write about anything you want. Forget the assignment sheet. Just make sure your paper's at least two full pages, and ... and that it's about something that matters to you."

His eyes widened in disbelief. "Anything?" he asked.

"Anything," I answered.

Afterward I worried that I'd violated the letter of the law set down by the English Department for freshman composition. But I consoled myself by arguing that I hadn't violated its spirit. I went on worrying about Robby and my response to him while I cooked dinner, did my laundry and fed the cat. A week later, after he handed in his next paper, I pulled it from the pile as soon as I sat down in my office, anxious to discover what he had to say. Neatly stapled together were six full pages of small, careful print. The first sentences were: "Kevin woke up with his face in the high grass beside the interstate. He could hear cars whizzing by and his head hurt. He'd blacked out again."

I looked up from the paper and felt my eyes begin to sting. Taking a long gulp of coffee, I kept reading. In a moving, concrete and straightforward style, Robby continued for six pages describing the life of a teenage alcoholic. "Kevin," he wrote, "hated looking into the mirror at himself. It made him want another beer." The Kevin that Robby described lost friends because of his drinking, woke up in places he couldn't remember arriving at, and made D's in chemistry, calculus and English. He felt "desperate, alone and sure of dying."

At his paper's conclusion, Robby added a postscript:

"Miss Bradford, this is not me. I wanted to try writing fiction, but I don't want you to think this is me." I pushed his paper aside, put my head on my desk and cried. All of the times my father had bellowed, "I don't have a drinking problem," replayed themselves on the screen of my thoughts.

I reached for a tissue. What should I do? If I referred Robby to the alcohol treatment program at Student Services, he wouldn't go. If I contacted his counselor at the General College, what would I say? That to every alcoholic his dependency is only fiction? That I had a way of knowing when people drank too much? That I'd grown up with an alcoholic father? That my younger brother had looked just like Robby his first year in college—the year he wrecked two cars and nearly killed himself? I knew I wasn't a counselor, a social worker or a psychiatrist, and I was sure Robby's presence in my class had been some kind of cosmic mistake. *I'm just an English teacher,* I thought. But the words stuck in my mind as if they contained the answer. *You* are *an English teacher. Just teach English the very best way you can.*

I poured another cup of coffee. Then, with an almost peaceful determination, I began grading the paper. Scrupulously I marked every misspelling or grammatical error, put in absent commas and suggested shorter paragraphs. Finally, in my end note I wrote, "Robby, this is your best paper yet. Concrete, compelling and interesting. You involve the reader in Kevin's painful, desperate situation. But fiction requires a conclusion. What happens to Kevin? Does he find help or end up a victim of the bottle? For your next paper, I'd like you to finish the story." I scrawled a large B below the note.

When I handed the papers back, Robby was in class, but he missed the two classes that followed. Panic crept over me at odd moments that week. Had I done something so wrong that he'd decided not to come back at all? How could I have imagined I could help such a confused, haunted teenager? I knew if he didn't show up for class the next time, I'd have to notify his adviser.

When I walked into my classroom on Monday morning, I immediately looked back at Robby's seat. It was empty. As I opened my book, I tried to squelch disappointment long enough to teach the other students.

Then, glancing up to take roll, my heart jumped. Robby was there after all, but not in his usual seat in the corner. He'd moved to the second row. His hair was combed, and he wore a bright-green polo shirt and crisp khaki pants. I'd never seen him in anything but torn jeans and an old shirt. Catching my gaze, he smiled broadly.

Back in my office an hour later I turned to the conclusion of Robby's "fictitious" narrative. He'd written a single paragraph: "I couldn't write it. I was afraid how it would end up. I'm not drinking anymore and I'm going to Alcoholics Anonymous.* I know I can finish this now—if I can just get an extension."

*If you want to know more about A.A., write to P.O. Box 459, Grand Central Station, New York, NY 10163, or look for the phone number listed in your local directory's white pages under A.A.

I wrote at the bottom of the sheet, "Extension granted."

I still saw Robby after he finished my class, taking away a B– as his course grade. Usually it was early in the morning. I'd be walking across campus, clutching a cup of coffee, not yet awake, and I'd hear him shouting exuberantly, "Hey, Miss Bradford, how's it goin'?"

Robby had needed the professionals he went looking for and found. But I'd been wrong in arrogantly declaring that *I* had nothing to give. He'd needed me to believe he could make the changes so important to his leading a healthy, productive life. My mother had been that believing person for my father and brother—to this day faithful members of Alcoholics Anonymous.

I thank God for using my classroom as one of the instruments in Robby's change. And I remember Robby at the beginning of each semester when I carefully pray, "God, send me students who need what I can give."

A Prayer, a Pledge and a Promise

JO GARDNER

I'd tossed and turned that Saturday night, unable to sleep. Part of the trouble was that my husband, Jim, and I were living in our daughter's house. The catering business we'd sunk everything into had failed. While we were getting back on our feet financially, Vicki had welcomed us into her home, but I felt uneasy about being there. And then too, I kept thinking about the meeting I had said I'd attend at church the next day.

Our new sanctuary was under construction that spring, yet not all the money to pay for it had been raised. I knew the elders would be calling for pledges at the meeting, and I hated that we had nothing to give. Strangely, as I lay there staring at the ceiling, the figure of $1,000 had flashed through my head—not once, but several times. It was so preposterous I'd almost laughed. *A thousand dollars. Imagine my pledging a thousand dollars!*

The next day at the meeting in the fellowship hall of

Escondido's Cathedral of the Valley, I hung my head and offered my apologies to God as I heard pledges being called out all around me. And, as I sat there, once more the figure of $1,000 danced strangely in my head.

Lord, I prayed, *if we had it, I'd give it to You.*

You can earn it, came the answer in my head.

But how? I asked. *I'm just a wife and mother. I have no training, no job, no money-making prospects.*

You have a talent.

No, Lord, I think the only thing I've ever done well is make quilts.

Then make Me a quilt. His words were even more distinct than the voices in the fellowship hall.

Before I knew what I was doing, I was on my feet saying stoutly, "I'll make a quilt! I know this is unusual, but I'll make a quilt and sell it, and whatever I get for it will go to the building fund."

"What do you think your quilt will bring?" someone asked.

"Four hundred, maybe five hundred dollars," I blurted.

"Who will give this lady five hundred dollars for her quilt?" the leader asked.

Across the room a woman named Lee Clarke, whom I knew faintly, stood up. "I'll give her five hundred dollars for it," she said.

"Oh, my goodness," I mumbled. It was dizzying. God had directed me to pledge a quilt, and now He had supplied a buyer.

I sank down in my seat, bowed my head and promised

God that only my very best work would be done on *His* quilt.

The meeting buzzed on around me. Others were now making offers of services as well as cash. Then I heard a voice above all the others say, "I think that quilt is worth a thousand dollars, and I'll give that."

I sprang to my feet. It was Lee Clarke again. She had raised her own bid! But how could that be? No one had bid against her, and how could she have known about the figure in my head?

As soon as the meeting was over, I rushed up to Lee. "Thank you, but one thousand dollars is a lot to pay for a quilt," I told her.

"Don't worry," she said breezily. "They probably get that and more over in those shops in Rancho Santa Fe."

Strange, I thought, *if Lee hadn't offered to buy it, I was going to sell it myself to one of those shops.* We made a date to discuss patterns and colors, and I left, half in wonderment, half in jubilation.

Lee selected a lovely open-fan design and chose colors of brown, cream and gold. As soon as Jim and I were able to relocate into our own house, I began quilting in earnest, working eight hours a day, three to five days a week. The work was going well, but the project was so enormous that sometimes it overwhelmed me.

During these times I often turned to prayer. I prayed for patience so that the quilt would be as near perfect as I could make it. As I stitched I asked God to be with all those who would use His quilt. I began to form a picture of a woman holding the quilt, cherishing it, and I prayed for her too.

The winter months melted together. By March I had all the patchwork pieced together, and I began lining the quilt. On March 15, 1984, I embroidered my name and the date on an upper corner of the lining. "It is finished, Lord," I said. "Let this quilt be a blessing to our church, and bless the home it goes into with peace and security."

The following Sunday, I gave the quilt to Lee. I asked her to hold one corner of it so I could open it up to full size.

"Oh," she whispered, "it's beautiful. It must have a million stitches in it." She didn't say much more, but she couldn't seem to take her eyes off it. I believed she was pleased with it, and I was happy because $1,000 had been added to my church's building fund.

Two months later, on an afternoon in May, I was returning from an errand when I spotted Lee on our front porch. She had the quilt in her arms.

"Is something the matter?" I asked her.

"Jo," she blurted, "I have to give this back to you."

I was stunned. "What's wrong with it?"

"I love it," she said softly, "but I cannot keep it. ... I have a feeling about it I can't explain. There is so much of you in it. Jo, this is *your* quilt. Please take it."

She pressed it into my hands.

"Jo," she said, "there is just one stipulation I want to make. Don't ever let this beautiful thing get out of your family. It must be part of your family's heritage."

"God bless you," I said. "Oh, Jo, God bless you." Then

she was gone, and I was sitting on the sofa, pressing the quilt to my chest. I had made many quilts, but never had I kept one for myself. Now God had given back to me the very quilt I had made for Him.

And then it came to me: The woman I had prayed for, the one I had pictured in my prayers—that woman was me. And the home I had asked God to bless with peace and security, that was my home, Jim's and mine. Truly our God is amazing. Just as the Bible verse promises: "Give, and it shall be given unto you; good measure, pressed down, and shaken together, and running over" (Luke 6:38).

Running over, like the quilt I held on my lap, turning gold in the late afternoon sun.

The Promise of Prayer

We know that prayer is a powerful force because we are praying to an Almighty God. Many of the stories in this book have focused on times when praying is extremely difficult. As we have witnessed, those are the times when it is necessary to give up our own ways, our own point of view, our own will, in order to enter the flow of God's blessing and power.

When we have been wronged and are asked to forgive the one who wronged us, when we are shown our true selves and must acknowledge our weaknesses and failures to God, when we come to the end of our own power and ability and must surrender everything to God—at these times God asks of us nothing less than our whole selves.

"Finally, be strong in the Lord and his mighty power.... And pray in the Spirit on all occasions with all kinds of prayer (Ephesians 6:20 niv). This is when you can truly experience a promise that is never broken: the power of prayer.